DELIVERANCE MINISTER'S HANDBOOK

A PRACTICAL GUIDE FOR FREEDOM MINISTRY

I0167891

DELIVERANCE MINISTER'S MANUAL

A PRACTICAL GUIDE FOR FREEDOM MINISTRY

THOMAS CORNELL

SOZO PUBLISHING

CONTENTS

INTRODUCTION

When we look through the pages of Scripture, one theme rises again and again: when God's people are in bondage, He raises up deliverers. Judges 2:16 says, "*Nevertheless, the Lord raised up judges, who delivered them out of the hand of those who plundered them.*" Again in Judges 3:9 we read, "*When the children of Israel cried out to the Lord, the Lord raised up a deliverer for the children of Israel, who delivered them...*" This was God's pattern: His people cry out under oppression, and He answers by raising up a man or woman filled with His Spirit and authority to bring freedom.

That image is central to this book. God is still raising up deliverers in our generation. The need for freedom has not diminished—it has increased. Our world is saturated with fear, anxiety, trauma, addiction, and demonic oppression. And God's answer is still the same: He raises up men and women to partner with Him in the ministry of deliverance.

God's Deliverers Through History

When we think of deliverance, one of the first names that comes to mind is Moses. God called him out of obscurity and said, *"Come now, and I will send you to Pharaoh that you may bring My people, the children of Israel, out of Egypt"* (Exodus 3:10). Moses was God's chosen deliverer for a nation. Through him, Israel was freed from slavery, Pharaoh was confronted, and the power of Egypt's gods was broken. Moses shows us that deliverance is not just about individual freedom—it's about breaking systemic oppression and releasing God's people to worship Him.

In the New Testament, we see a powerful picture in Philip's ministry to Samaria. Acts 8:5–8 says, *"Then Philip went down to the city of Samaria and preached Christ to them. And the multitudes with one accord heeded the things spoken by Philip, hearing and seeing the miracles which he did. For unclean spirits, crying with a loud voice, came out of many who were possessed; and many who were paralyzed and lame were healed. And there was great joy in that city."* Notice the result: when demons were cast out and bodies were healed, an entire city was marked by joy. Deliverance is not just a side ministry—it is central to revival.

And, of course, Jesus Himself is the ultimate Deliverer. He declared in Luke 4:18, *"The Spirit of the Lord is upon Me, because He has anointed Me to preach the gospel to the poor; He has sent Me to heal the brokenhearted, to proclaim liberty to the captives and recovery of sight to the blind, to set at liberty those who are oppressed."* His ministry was marked by casting out demons, healing the sick, and proclaiming the Kingdom. Everywhere Jesus went, darkness had to flee. Colossians 1:13 tells us that *"He has delivered us from the power of darkness and conveyed us into the kingdom of the Son of His love."*

This is the model: God raised up Moses for Israel, Philip for

Samaria, Jesus as the Deliverer of all—and now He raises up you and me to carry on this ministry in His name.

The Mandate of the Church

Deliverance is not optional. It is not a side project for a few "specialists." It is part of the Great Commission. Jesus said in Mark 16:17, "*And these signs will follow those who believe: In My name they will cast out demons.*" Casting out demons is not an advanced ministry for the elite—it is the inheritance of every believer.

Yet while every believer carries authority in Christ, not every believer is ready to minister deliverance in a healthy and safe way. That's where this manual comes in. My heart is to provide you with a practical, biblical, Spirit-led guide to equip you as a deliverance minister.

This book is not written to entertain curiosity or sensationalize the demonic. It is written to train and prepare men and women of God to set captives free. Deliverance is not about chasing demons—it is about exalting Jesus and establishing His Kingdom in people's lives.

Why Preparation Matters

I need to say something at the outset: deliverance is not a ministry you should run into after your first breakthrough. In the church I lead, I do not release people to minister deliverance until their second year in our School of Ministry. Why? Because the first year is about receiving healing, deliverance, and identity. You cannot freely give what you have not freely received. Even Jesus' disciples were not sent to cast out demons until Matthew 10, after they had walked with Him, been healed, delivered, and discipled.

That is why I emphasize foundations. Deliverance ministers must be:

- People who have experienced healing and deliverance themselves.
- People who are rooted in the local church and living under covering.
- People who are committed to holiness, humility, and intimacy with Jesus.

If you rush into deliverance ministry without these foundations, you will burn out, get deceived, or open yourself up to attack. On the other hand, if you take the time to let God heal you, deliver you, and root you, you will carry authority, compassion, and wisdom that produces lasting fruit.

Humility and Authority

Another tension we must hold is between humility and authority. On one hand, some people feel timid about deliverance. They think, "Who am I to command demons?" But the truth is, you are seated with Christ in heavenly places (Ephesians 2:6). You carry His Spirit and His authority. Demons do not respond to your personality—they respond to the Christ in you.

On the other hand, some people swing to pride. When demons start screaming, saying things like, "I hate you... why are there so many angels with you?" it can be tempting to think you are something special. But never forget—it is only by His grace. Your authority is borrowed authority. Pride is the fastest way to fall.

Humility is not thinking less of yourself; it is recognizing that your power is Christ in you. You are powerful—not because you are all that, but because He is all that, and He lives in you. This book will keep pointing you back to that balance.

Practical Language for Deliverance

One of the things I want to give you in this manual is practical language. Many people feel lost in a deliverance session because they don't know what to say. Should they yell? Should they pray quietly? Should they ask questions?

This book will equip you with clear, direct language you can use in the moment of ministry. Phrases like:

- "I command the spirit of anxiety and all of its kingdom to leave now in Jesus' name."
- "I bind the spirit of infirmity and its kingdom and command you to go to the pit."
- "I break every generational curse of addiction and command every spirit connected to it to leave."

These are not formulas—they are examples of the kind of authoritative, Spirit-led language that flows out of Scripture and the finished work of the cross.

The Role of Discernment

We will also talk about how the discerning of spirits operates. Sometimes it comes as a thought, sometimes as a feeling in your body, sometimes as a shift in atmosphere. For example, when laying hands on someone influenced by witchcraft, I have at times felt a sharp, needle-like sensation in my fingertips. That's the Holy Spirit alerting me to what's operating. Other times, the person will suddenly manifest, or the Spirit will give me an impression of a name or memory.

Discernment is not about guessing—it is about recognizing the Spirit's signals and responding with authority. This manual will help you grow in recognizing those signals and acting with clarity.

Why Community and Aftercare Matter

Deliverance is not the finish line—it is the starting line. Once a person is set free, they must be discipled into lasting freedom. In the church I lead, that means connecting them into a House Church—a spiritual family led by mature, trained disciples who can walk with them in prayer, healing, deliverance, and discipleship.

If you cast demons out but don't root someone in the house of God, you've only done half the job. Jesus said in Matthew 12:43–45 that if a spirit leaves but the house is left empty, it comes back with seven more. That's why aftercare matters so much.

How to Use This Manual

Think of this book as both a training manual and a field guide. It will give you the theology, the principles, and the practices. It will also give you the practical tools—sample prayers, ministry checklists, and clear commands you can use in real sessions.

If you are brand new, let this manual guide you into serving as a helper first. Don't rush to lead. Watch, learn, pray, and ask questions afterward. Apprenticeship is the safest way to grow.

If you are a seasoned minister, let this manual sharpen and refresh you. None of us ever arrive. The enemy is crafty, and the Spirit is always teaching us more.

If you are a pastor or leader, use this manual to train your teams. Deliverance should not be limited to one or two "specialists" in the church. It should be part of the normal ministry of Jesus flowing through His body.

Deliverance is about Jesus. It is about the cross, the resurrection, and the power of the Spirit. Demons may scream, but they are defeated. Your job is not to glorify the demonic, but to exalt Christ as Deliverer.

My prayer is that as you read this manual, you will catch the heart of God for freedom, and you will step into your calling as a deliverer in this generation. May you walk in humility, authority, wisdom, and love. And may you see the joy of captives being set free, just like Philip did in Samaria, until entire cities are filled with joy.

THE CALL AND CHARACTER OF A DELIVERANCE MINISTER

THE MINISTRY OF DELIVERANCE IS NOT FIRST ABOUT POWER, IT'S about character. Anyone can shout at a demon. But not everyone carries the authority of Jesus in a way that makes demons tremble. Authority is not found in volume or personality—it is found in a life that is surrendered to Christ and shaped by His Spirit. Before we talk about casting out demons, we must talk about the kind of person God can trust to carry this ministry.

Deliverance is a holy assignment. It requires men and women who are consecrated to the Lord, submitted to His Word, and walking under His covering. This chapter will lay out the essential qualities of a deliverance minister: holiness, humility, prayer, submission, and a rejection of pride, fear, and performance.

The Call of a Deliverance Minister

Deliverance ministry is not something we choose for ourselves. It is a calling from God. Judges says that the Lord "raised up deliverers" for His people (Judges 2:16). In other words, God Himself chose and equipped people for this work. In the same way, deliverance ministers today are raised up by the Spirit.

This doesn't mean you need a dramatic angelic visitation to qualify. It means that as you walk with Jesus, receive freedom yourself, and stay faithful in His house, He begins to entrust you with His authority. Over time, you discover that when you pray for people, things break off. You see oppression lift. You feel a burden for the bound. That is the Spirit's call.

If you are reading this manual, I believe you are sensing that call. My encouragement is this: treat it as sacred. Don't treat deliverance like a hobby or a side project. It is holy work. And if God has called you, He will also shape your character to carry it.

Holiness: Living Set Apart

Holiness is not optional for a deliverance minister. Demons recognize whether a vessel is clean or compromised. Remember Acts 19, when the sons of Sceva tried to cast out demons by saying, "We adjure you by the Jesus whom Paul preaches"? The demons replied, "Jesus I know, and Paul I know; but who are you?" (v. 15). And they left those men beaten and naked. Why? Because the sons of Sceva tried to use borrowed language without living a consecrated life.

Authority flows from holiness. A life set apart to God becomes a channel for His power. Holiness doesn't mean perfection, but it does mean integrity. It means you keep short accounts with God, you walk in repentance, and you refuse to live with hidden sin.

As a deliverance minister, you will confront spirits of lust, addiction, greed, and deception. If those things are secretly active in your own life, you are vulnerable. Jesus said, "The ruler of this world is coming, and he has nothing in Me" (John 14:30). That is our goal—that when the enemy comes to look for a foothold, he finds nothing in us.

Holiness is about more than what you avoid; it's about what you pursue. Pursue purity of heart, purity of speech, purity of motives. Set your eyes on Jesus, let His Word wash you, and live in a way that makes room for His presence.

Humility: Staying Low Before God

Humility is the soil where authority grows. In deliverance ministry, you will experience moments where demons scream, manifestations break out, and people look to you for leadership. It is tempting to let that attention feed your pride. But never forget—this is not about you. It is about Jesus, the Deliverer.

Demons sometimes try to flatter. I've had spirits shout things like, "We hate you, Apostle Tom! Why are there so many angels with you?" That's a trap. If you let those words shape your identity, pride will creep in. Your authority does not come from demons recognizing you. It comes from you being hidden in Christ.

On the other hand, demons will also try to intimidate. They'll say, "We are stronger than you" or "You can't cast us out." That's another lie. I remember once confronting a spirit that said it was more powerful than me. I replied, "The Bible says I am seated with Christ in heavenly places, and your throne is not higher than His throne." The demon responded,

"You're right. I'm a liar." Authority flows from humility rooted in Scripture, not arrogance.

True humility is not thinking less of yourself; it is thinking rightly about yourself. You are powerful because Christ lives in you. You are nothing without Him, but in Him, you are more than a conqueror.

Prayer Life: Walking in the Spirit

A deliverance minister must be a person of prayer. You cannot learn this ministry from books alone. You must live in constant fellowship with the Holy Spirit.

Prayer keeps you sensitive. Often, discernment comes not in the session but in your private time with God. He may show you in prayer the strongholds a person is dealing with, or He may warn you about an attack coming against you. Prayer sharpens your discernment.

Prayer also keeps you covered. Deliverance is warfare. When you cast out demons, you're striking at the kingdom of darkness. If you're not prayed up, you're vulnerable. But when you live in prayer, you live under the shadow of the Almighty (Psalm 91).

Finally, prayer keeps you humble. It reminds you that the power is not yours. Every victory in deliverance belongs to Jesus. Prayer keeps you in dependence on Him.

Submission to Authority

Deliverance ministers must walk under spiritual covering. Lone rangers are dangerous in this ministry. When you are submitted to leaders in the house of God, you carry their covering into battle. That covering is like spiritual air support—it protects you, grounds you, and keeps you safe.

In my church, I never release someone into deliverance ministry without first testing their submission. Can they serve? Can they receive correction? Can they stay rooted in the house? If not, they are not ready. Authority is not given to the independent; it is given to the submitted.

Even Jesus walked under authority. He said, "I do nothing of Myself; but as My Father taught Me, I speak these things" (John 8:28). If Jesus modeled submission, how much more should we?

Avoiding Pride, Fear, and Performance

Three traps will derail a deliverance minister if not confronted: pride, fear, and performance.

Pride says, "Look at me. I have power over demons." That's the fastest way to lose authority. Pride caused Lucifer to fall, and it will cause you to fall too. Stay low. Remember whose power you carry.

Fear says, "What if I fail? What if the demons don't listen?" Fear paralyzes. It makes you shrink back when you should step forward. Fear is a lie. Jesus has already won the victory. When you stand in His name, demons must obey.

Performance says, "I need to prove something. I need to show people I'm powerful." That turns ministry into a show. Deliverance is not about performance. It's about love. The goal is not for you to look anointed but for the person to walk free.

Pride, fear, and performance all shift the focus to you. True ministry keeps the focus on Jesus.

The Fruit of Character

When you walk in holiness, humility, prayer, and submission, something beautiful happens: you carry authority without striving. You don't have to yell, posture, or pretend. When you say, "Go," demons go—not because of you, but because of the Christ you carry.

People will sense it. They'll feel safe around you. They'll know you're not there to control them, but to serve them. And demons will know it too.

This is why character matters more than technique. You can memorize all the prayers and commands in this manual, but if your character is compromised, it won't matter. Authority flows from intimacy, humility, and holiness.

A Final Word on the Call

You are not called to be a superstar deliverance minister. You are called to be a servant of Jesus who sets captives free. That means walking in purity, staying humble, living in prayer, and staying covered.

If you will cultivate these qualities, God will trust you with greater authority. And you will see lives changed, families restored, and even cities transformed.

Remember: the Lord raises up deliverers. He raised up Moses. He raised up Philip. He raised up judges in Israel. He raised up Jesus as the Deliverer of all. And now He is raising up you. Walk worthy of the call.

Reflection Questions

1. IN THIS CHAPTER WE LEARN THAT AUTHORITY IN DELIVERANCE flows from holiness, humility, and intimacy—not personality or volume. Which of these character qualities do you feel God is highlighting in your life right now, and why? How might a lack in that area affect your spiritual authority?

2. THE CHAPTER TEACHES THAT DEMONS RECOGNIZE WHETHER A vessel is clean or compromised. What areas of "hidden life" (thought patterns, habits, motives) tend to become footholds for the enemy, and what does it look like to pursue holiness not just in behavior but in the heart?

3. DELIVERANCE MINISTERS MUST WALK UNDER SPIRITUAL covering. How have you seen submission to spiritual authority either strengthen or challenge your maturity? What might submission practically look like for someone who senses a call into deliverance ministry?

2

FOUNDATIONS OF PREPARATION

DELIVERANCE IS POWERFUL MINISTRY, BUT IT IS ALSO DANGEROUS when mishandled. It is one of the clearest demonstrations of the Kingdom of God clashing with the kingdom of darkness. When we step into this ministry, we are not stepping into something light or casual—we are confronting demonic powers that have held people captive for years, sometimes for generations. Because of this, the preparation of the minister is as important as the ministry itself.

I want to say this clearly: before you try to deliver others, you must allow the Lord to deliver you. Before you start pulling strongholds out of others, you must let Him tear them down in your own life. This is why I call this chapter "foundations." If the foundation of your own life is cracked, shaky, or undeveloped, then when the storms of battle come, you won't last. But if your foundation is strong, you will stand, and you will minister from a place of stability, confidence, and authority in Christ.

Receiving Healing and Deliverance Yourself

The first preparation for deliverance ministry is this: you must first go through your own inner healing and deliverance journey. You cannot give away what you don't carry. Jesus said in Matthew 10:8, "Freely you have received, freely give." Notice the order—first we receive, then we give.

I've seen this mistake too often. Someone gets a taste of freedom, and immediately they want to go and cast out demons in others. The problem is that their own foundation isn't secure yet. They've been delivered from one area, but they haven't renewed their mind, healed from their wounds, or walked through repentance in other areas. Instead of carrying authority, they carry zeal without wisdom. And zeal without wisdom can do damage.

In the church I lead, this is why we don't release people into deliverance ministry until the second year of our School of Ministry. The first year is focused on identity, healing, and deliverance. We walk people through their own process of being restored in Christ before ever teaching them how to minister freedom to others. Only after they have received deeply do we allow them to give.

If you are going to be effective in deliverance ministry, you must let the Holy Spirit go deep in you. Deal with your wounds. Receive forgiveness. Renounce inner vows. Break unhealthy soul ties. Walk through repentance and cleansing. Learn to forgive those who have hurt you. Let Jesus be the Deliverer in your own life first. This does two things: it closes doors the enemy might exploit in you, and it gives you compassion for those you will minister to.

Renewing the Mind

Deliverance is not just about casting out demons; it is about renewing the mind. Romans 12:2 says, "Do not be conformed to this world, but be transformed by the renewing of your mind." If a person receives deliverance but doesn't renew their thinking, the same demonic patterns will find an open door again.

The same is true for ministers. You cannot minister freedom with a worldly mindset. You must let God's Word reshape how you think about identity, holiness, authority, and power. Renewing the mind means replacing lies with truth. It means aligning every thought with Christ.

As a deliverance minister, you will often find yourself confronting lies in others. Lies like: "I'll never be free." "God doesn't love me." "This addiction defines me." You cannot confront lies in others if you are still bound by them yourself. You must let the Word of God rewire your thinking until you know who you are in Christ and whose authority you carry.

Living Holy

Holiness is not optional. I touched on this in the last chapter, but it bears repeating. If you are dabbling in compromise— entertaining pornography, walking in bitterness, cutting corners in integrity—you are building cracks in your armor. Demons will exploit those cracks.

Living holy is not about legalism; it's about protection. Holiness keeps your spirit sharp. It keeps you sensitive to the Spirit. It allows you to carry God's presence with weight and authority.

If you want to be trusted with authority over darkness, then live a life that is set apart to God. Keep your heart pure. Guard your eyes and ears. Walk in humility. Stay accountable. Deliverance is a holy ministry, and it requires holy vessels.

Rooted in the Local Church

One of the greatest mistakes in deliverance ministry is trying to do it apart from the local church. I've seen people who have zeal for casting out demons but no connection to spiritual family. They float from place to place, ministering deliverance without accountability. This is dangerous—for them and for the people they minister to.

Deliverance must flow from the house of God. In the church I lead, I make sure every deliverance minister is rooted in our spiritual family, submitted to leadership, and accountable to others. Why? Because authority flows through covering. A lone ranger may cast out a demon here or there, but they will eventually burn out, get deceived, or cause harm. But a minister rooted in the house, covered by leaders, and surrounded by family will be protected, corrected, and strengthened.

If you want to be effective in deliverance, don't just read this manual and launch out on your own. Stay planted in your local church. Serve faithfully. Walk in submission. Let your leaders know what you are doing. Covering is not control; it is protection.

Covering and Accountability

Let me press this point a little further. Deliverance stirs up warfare. When you cast out demons, you stir the hornet's nest of the enemy's camp. If you are not under covering, you are exposing yourself to unnecessary attack.

Accountability is your shield. When you have leaders who can correct you, pray for you, and stand with you, you are safer. When you have a team around you, you are stronger. When you are transparent about your own struggles, you close the enemy's access points.

Authority without accountability is dangerous. But authority under covering is powerful. Even Jesus walked under His Father's authority. He said, "The Son can do nothing of Himself, but what He sees the Father do" (John 5:19). If Jesus modeled submission, how much more should we?

Jesus' Model in Matthew 10

It is no accident that Jesus did not release His disciples into deliverance ministry until Matthew 10. By that point, they had walked with Him, watched Him minister, and received from Him. They had been healed, taught, corrected, and discipled. Only then did He say, "And when He had called His twelve disciples to Him, He gave them power over unclean spirits, to cast them out" (v. 1).

Notice: the disciples were first receivers before they were givers. They didn't go from broken fishermen straight into casting out demons. They walked with Jesus, grew in intimacy, learned His ways, and then He released them.

This is still the model today. Don't rush. Be willing to spend a season as a learner, as a disciple, as a helper. Then, in time, God will entrust you with more.

Balancing the Timid and the Overconfident

As I train deliverance ministers, I often see two extremes.

On one end, there are those who are timid. They fear stepping out. They think, "Who am I to command demons?" On the other end, there are those who are overconfident. They want to rush in headfirst, thinking they are untouchable.

Both extremes are dangerous. The timid must remember: it is not about your strength; it is about Christ's authority. Demons don't respond to your personality; they respond to the name of Jesus. You may feel weak, but He is strong in you. When you step out in faith, He will back you up.

The overconfident must remember: this is not about you. Authority is borrowed. It is by His grace alone. Pride is deadly in this ministry. If you think you are invincible, you are setting yourself up for a fall.

The balance is this: confidence in Christ, humility in yourself. Boldness rooted in Him, dependence that keeps you on your knees.

True Humility: Christ in Me

This leads us to the foundation of all preparation: true humility. True humility is not saying, "I am weak, I am nothing, I have no authority." That's false humility. True humility says, "I am nothing without Christ, but in Him, I am powerful."

Paul said in Galatians 2:20, "It is no longer I who live, but Christ lives in me." That is the foundation. Deliverance is not about who you are in the flesh; it is about who you are in Christ.

When you walk into a deliverance session, you don't walk in alone. You walk in with Jesus living in you, the Spirit empowering you, and the Father covering you. That is humility and confidence together.

Building the Foundation

If you take nothing else from this chapter, take this: deliverance ministry is not about rushing into battle with a sword swinging wildly. It is about letting God build a strong foundation in you.

- Receive healing and deliverance yourself.
- Let your mind be renewed by the Word.
- Live holy and set apart.
- Stay rooted in the local church.
- Walk under covering and accountability.
- Follow Jesus' model—receive before you give.
- Stay balanced: bold in Christ, humble in yourself.

If you build this foundation, you will last. If you skip this foundation, you will crumble.

The enemy doesn't fear loud voices; he fears holy vessels. He doesn't tremble at passion alone; he trembles at those who are hidden in Christ, walking in humility, authority, and holiness.

So let the Lord prepare you. Let Him build you. Let Him shape your character. Because when He does, you will be able to stand, and you will be able to deliver others—not out of zeal alone, but out of authority and wisdom that flows from a life surrendered to Jesus.

Reflection Questions

1. THIS CHAPTER EMPHASIZES THAT BEFORE WE DELIVER OTHERS, we must first allow Jesus to deliver us. Where in your life do you sense the Holy Spirit inviting you into deeper healing, repentance, or renewal? What doors need to be closed, wounds healed, or lies replaced before you can minister freedom with integrity and authority?

2. DELIVERANCE MINISTRY REQUIRES A RENEWED MIND AND submission to spiritual covering. In what areas does your thinking still mirror the world rather than the Word? And how does your relationship with church leadership—submission, accountability, rootedness—strengthen or hinder your readiness to step into spiritual warfare?

3. THIS CHAPTER WARNS AGAINST TWO EXTREMES: FEAR (TIMIDITY) and pride (overconfidence). Which tendency do you naturally lean toward, and why? What does healthy, Christ-centered confidence look like for you personally as you consider ministering deliverance?

3

DISCERNMENT, WISDOM, AND BOUNDARIES

IF DELIVERANCE MINISTRY IS A BATTLE, THEN DISCERNMENT IS your radar, wisdom is your strategy, and boundaries are your safeguards. Too many people rush into this ministry with zeal but no radar, no strategy, and no safeguards—and that is how they burn out, get deceived, or cause harm.

This chapter will equip you with the essentials of discernment, wisdom, and boundaries so that you can minister deliverance safely, effectively, and under the leadership of the Holy Spirit.

The Role of the Holy Spirit and the Gifts

The Holy Spirit is the Deliverer. You are simply His vessel. If you forget that, you will either lean on your flesh or fall into striving. The Spirit is the one who gives discernment, exposes lies, reveals strongholds, and empowers your words.

Paul lists spiritual gifts in 1 Corinthians 12, and three of them are especially vital for deliverance:

1. The discerning of spirits. This is not suspicion or guesswork—it is the supernatural ability to perceive what spirit is at work, whether demonic, angelic, or human. It allows you to cut through confusion and recognize the root of what you're confronting.

2. The word of knowledge. This is when the Spirit gives you insight into a situation you could not know naturally. For example, you may suddenly know the age when a wound occurred, or sense the specific door that opened to a demon's activity.

3. Prophecy. Prophecy calls people into their identity and future. Sometimes in deliverance, the Spirit will not only cast something out but also speak destiny into the person, sealing their freedom with hope and vision.

These gifts do not operate apart from Scripture—they align with the Word. But they give us real-time guidance in the heat of ministry.

Ways the Discerning of Spirits Operates

Every minister learns over time how the Holy Spirit alerts them to demonic activity. It is rarely the same for everyone. Here are some common ways discerning of spirits operates:

- Physical sensations. You may feel pressure in your chest, a stabbing pain, heat in your hands, or even a tingling like needles in your fingertips when laying hands on someone. For example, when confronting witchcraft, I have at times felt sharp pinpricks in my fingers—an alert that witchcraft was active.
- Impressions or sudden knowing. You may simply "know" what spirit is present without anyone telling

you. This inner impression comes like a thought but carries weight and authority.

- Atmospheric shifts. Sometimes the entire room shifts. You may feel heaviness, confusion, or even sudden fear that wasn't there before. That's often an indicator that a spirit is manifesting in the atmosphere.
- Emotional shifts. You may suddenly feel anger, sadness, or anxiety that isn't your own. This is often the Spirit letting you sense what is inside the person.
- Visions or mental pictures. Some receive quick flashes or images—like seeing chains, darkness, or a snake wrapped around someone. These visions give clues to what is happening in the spirit.
- Vocal manifestations. At times, the spirit itself will manifest and speak. We'll cover that more in Chapter 8, but discerning of spirits allows you to recognize when it is a spirit speaking and not just the person.

None of these are formulas. Discernment is a relationship. The more time you spend with the Spirit, the more you'll recognize His nudges and signals.

Always Ministering with Another Person Present

Deliverance should rarely, if ever, be done alone. Jesus sent His disciples out two by two (Mark 6:7). Why? Because ministry is safer and more effective with partnership.

When you minister with another person present:

- You have accountability—no one can accuse you of impropriety.

- You have agreement—your prayers are multiplied.
- You have covering—when you grow tired, someone else can step in.
- You have protection—if manifestations become physical, someone else is there to help.

Ministering alone makes you vulnerable to accusation, deception, and exhaustion. Always bring another trusted, trained person with you.

Roles of the Lead Minister vs. Helper/Witness

When two people minister together, it is important to clarify roles:

- The Lead Minister is the one directing the session. They ask the questions, give the commands, and carry the main authority in the moment. Their focus is on the person receiving ministry and on listening to the Holy Spirit for direction.
- The Helper/Witness is not a passive observer—they have vital responsibilities:

  - Praying silently in agreement.
  - Listening for anything the Spirit might reveal.
  - Watching the person's body language or manifestations.
  - Recording notes if needed for follow-up.
  - Providing safety if the person becomes physically agitated.
  - Afterward, praying a covering prayer over the minister and the recipient.

The Helper is not there to take over, contradict, or compete.

Their role is to support and strengthen. A good helper multiplies the authority of the lead minister by staying in unity.

The Apprenticeship Principle

One of the safest and most effective ways to grow in deliverance ministry is through apprenticeship. Before you step into the role of Lead Minister, you should first serve as a Helper/Witness for a season.

As a helper, you learn more by watching and praying than you ever could from just reading about deliverance. You see how seasoned ministers discern spirits, how they respond to manifestations, how they lead people in repentance, and how they maintain authority. You can ask questions afterward, reflect on what happened, and grow in understanding without the pressure of leading.

Too often, someone reads a book or attends a single training and immediately wants to lead deliverance. That is reckless. This manual can equip you with knowledge, but wisdom comes from walking alongside someone seasoned.

In my church, I always encourage new ministers to start as helpers. Serve, pray, watch, and learn. Let it get in your spirit. Then, when the time comes, God will release you to lead—but by then, you'll be steady, wise, and trained.

Gender Considerations and Safety

We must also be wise about gender dynamics in deliverance. It is best practice for men to minister deliverance to men and women to women, whenever possible. At the very least, always have someone of the same gender present in the room.

This is not just about appearance—it is about protection. Deliverance can involve physical manifestations, tears, deep emotional moments, and even resurfaced memories of trauma. If boundaries are not clear, the enemy can twist things and bring accusation.

Set clear standards in your ministry: never be alone with someone of the opposite sex in deliverance, never touch someone inappropriately, and always keep things in the light. This protects the integrity of the ministry and keeps the focus on Jesus.

Post-Session Debrief and Prayer

After every deliverance session, it is wise to pause for debrief and covering prayer. This serves three purposes:

1. For the recipient. Take time to pray blessing, peace, and the infilling of the Holy Spirit over them. Make sure they are calm, stable, and encouraged before they leave. Sometimes the most important part of deliverance is not the casting out but the building up afterward.
2. For the team. Take a moment with your helper to discuss what happened. What did you sense? What worked well? What could be done differently? Ask the Spirit for clarity. This debrief sharpens both of you for future ministry.
3. For covering. Close in prayer for protection. Ask the Lord to seal the work, cover everyone involved, and block any retaliation from the enemy. Always end with thanksgiving and worship, reminding yourself that the glory belongs to Jesus alone.

Walking in Wisdom

Discernment shows you what is happening. Wisdom shows you how to respond. Boundaries keep you safe while you respond. Together, these qualities make a deliverance minister effective for the long haul.

Do not rush. Stay humble. Learn to listen to the Spirit. Grow as a helper before you lead. Keep your ministry safe through wise boundaries. And always close in prayer and covering.

If you will cultivate discernment, wisdom, and boundaries, you will not only minister deliverance effectively—you will last in this ministry for years to come.

Reflection Questions

1. THIS CHAPTER TEACHES THAT DISCERNMENT OPERATES differently in every minister—through physical sensations, atmosphere shifts, inner knowing, or visions. How does the Holy Spirit most often speak to *you*, and what patterns have you noticed in how you sense spiritual activity? How confident are you in recognizing the difference between your emotions and the Spirit's alerts?

2. DELIVERANCE REQUIRES CLEAR BOUNDARIES SUCH AS NEVER ministering alone, honoring gender safety, and walking in accountability. Which boundaries do you feel strongest in, and which ones do you tend to overlook or underestimate? What safeguards do you need to put in place now to ensure long-term safety, purity, and effectiveness in ministry?

3. THIS CHAPTER EMPHASIZES THE IMPORTANCE OF SERVING AS A helper before becoming a lead minister. How do you personally respond to the idea of apprenticeship—does it feel like humility, restraint, irritation, or protection? What might God be forming in your character through a season of watching, learning, and supporting before stepping into leadership?

4

RECOGNIZING AND CLOSING OPEN DOORS

ONE OF THE MOST IMPORTANT PRINCIPLES IN DELIVERANCE ministry is understanding open doors. Demons don't just wander into people's lives at random—they look for access points. Scripture calls these "footholds" (Ephesians 4:27 NIV). When a door is open, the enemy has a legal right to enter. If you cast out a spirit but leave the door open, the person will not stay free. That is why discernment and wisdom are required, not just authority.

Deliverance is not just about commanding demons to leave —it's about identifying, closing, and renouncing the doors that gave them access in the first place. When the door is shut, the enemy loses his legal ground, and deliverance becomes lasting, not temporary.

Sin: The Most Obvious Door

The most obvious open door to demonic activity is sin. Romans 6:16 says, "Do you not know that to whom you present yourselves slaves to obey, you are that one's slaves whom you obey, whether of sin leading to death, or of obedience leading to righteousness?" Sin is not just disobedience—it is an agreement with the kingdom of darkness.

When a person chooses sin—whether sexual immorality, addiction, hatred, lying, or anything else—they are in effect opening a spiritual door and inviting the enemy in. If sin is unconfessed and unrepented, it becomes a landing strip for demonic influence.

As a deliverance minister, one of your main jobs is to help people renounce and repent of sin. Demons cling to sin like parasites cling to wounds. When the wound is cleansed by repentance, the parasites lose their grip. That's why repentance always precedes lasting freedom.

Trauma: The Unwanted Door

Not every door is opened by willful sin. Trauma is another common access point. Abuse, abandonment, betrayal, accidents, or shocking events can create deep wounds in the soul. Demons look for those wounds to exploit.

For example, a child who is abused may internalize lies like "I am worthless" or "I am unsafe." Those lies become entry points for spirits of rejection, fear, or shame. Trauma does not mean the person is guilty—it means they are vulnerable.

This is where the ministry of inner healing and deliverance overlap. Jesus not only casts out demons; He heals the brokenhearted (Luke 4:18). Often, the door of trauma must be addressed by inviting Jesus into the wound, breaking the lie, and releasing His truth. Once the wound is healed, the demon loses its place.

Unforgiveness: The Poisoned Door

Unforgiveness is one of the most common and stubborn open doors. Jesus was clear in Matthew 18:34–35: the unforgiving servant was handed over to tormentors because he refused to forgive. When we hold on to bitterness, resentment, or hatred, we are giving demons legal ground.

I tell people often: forgiveness is not optional if you want freedom. You cannot be delivered while holding onto bitterness. Forgiveness is not saying what happened was okay. It is releasing the person into God's hands and refusing to carry the weight anymore.

In deliverance sessions, I almost always lead people through forgiveness prayers. When they forgive from the heart, the door slams shut on tormenting spirits, and freedom comes quickly.

Inner Vows: The Binding Door

Inner vows are promises people make in moments of pain. A child neglected may say, "I will never depend on anyone again." A teenager betrayed may say, "I'll never let anyone get close to me." These vows feel protective, but they actually become prisons.

Inner vows are demonic agreements. They give the enemy permission to reinforce lies and build strongholds. For example, the vow "I'll never trust again" becomes an open door for spirits of fear, isolation, and control.

In deliverance, it is crucial to lead people to renounce inner vows. Once they break agreement with those lies and declare God's truth, the enemy's grip is broken.

Generational Curses: The Inherited Door

Exodus 20:5 speaks of the sins of the fathers visiting the children to the third and fourth generation. This is what we call generational curses—patterns of sin, addiction, sickness, or oppression that repeat in families.

If alcoholism, divorce, abuse, or occult practices run in the bloodline, you can be sure demonic influence is operating generationally. These spirits claim legal rights through family covenants or unrepented sin.

The good news is that the cross breaks every curse. Galatians 3:13 says Christ became a curse for us so that we could inherit blessing. In deliverance, have people renounce generational sins and declare their new identity in Christ. This closes inherited doors and ends cycles that have plagued families for generations.

Soul Ties and Ungodly Covenants

A soul tie is a deep emotional or spiritual connection that allows transfer of influence. God designed healthy soul ties—like marriage or family—to bond people in love. But when soul ties form through sin, they become demonic access points.
Examples include:

- Sexual relationships outside of marriage.
- Codependent or controlling friendships.
- Manipulative spiritual leaders.

Ungodly covenants work the same way. People make agreements, knowingly or unknowingly, with darkness—through vows, rituals, or even careless words. These covenants become contracts in the spirit realm that demons enforce.

Deliverance requires breaking ungodly soul ties and covenants. This is done through repentance, renunciation, and declaring the blood of Jesus as the only covenant over their life.

Occult Involvement: The Dangerous Door

Occult practices are one of the strongest open doors. Witchcraft, fortune telling, astrology, Ouija boards, New Age practices, and secret societies all invite demonic influence.

Deuteronomy 18:10–12 lists these practices and calls them detestable to the Lord. When someone engages in the occult, they are entering into agreement with spirits of witchcraft, divination, or sorcery. These spirits often bring torment, confusion, nightmares, or oppression.

Occult doors must be broken decisively. In deliverance, lead the person to renounce every involvement, destroy any objects tied to the occult, and declare Jesus as Lord. Once the covenant is broken, the spirits lose their ground.

Best Practice: The Set Free Process

In my ministry, I've found it most effective to lead people through a process of repentance, forgiveness, and renunciation before deliverance even begins. That's why I put together the Set Free material—a resource full of prayers that deal with open doors.

When someone takes the time to pray through forgiveness, renounce inner vows, break generational curses, and repent for sin and occult involvement, the actual deliverance session flows much smoother. The doors are already closed, so when you command demons to leave, they have no choice but to go.

That's why, whenever possible, I encourage ministers to give people this material in advance. Have them pray through it. Walk them through it. Set the stage for deliverance by addressing the legal rights first.

Flexibility: When Deliverance Must Happen Immediately

But we must also be flexible. Sometimes you don't have the luxury of preparation. A person might begin manifesting in a service, at the altar, or even on the street. In those moments, you don't stop and hand them a 50-page booklet. You act.

If deliverance must happen immediately, you deal with each open door as it comes up. If the spirit says, "I have the right of unforgiveness," then you lead the person to forgive right then. If it says, "Generational covenant," then you walk them through renouncing it on the spot. It may take longer, but it works.

The principle is simple: whenever possible, close the doors first through preparation. But when necessary, close them in the moment. Either way, doors must be shut for freedom to be lasting.

Practical Tips for Identifying Open Doors

Here are some practical ways to identify and close open doors in deliverance sessions:

1. Ask questions in assessment. Before ministry, ask about family history, trauma, patterns of sin, or occult involvement. This often reveals doors.
2. Listen for key words. People will often describe symptoms that point to open doors—"I feel rejected," "I can't stop this addiction," "It runs in my family."
3. Pay attention to discernment. Sometimes the Spirit will give you a sudden knowing or impression about a door, even if the person hasn't mentioned it.
4. Watch for manifestations. Certain demons react strongly when their door is mentioned. If unforgiveness is the door, you may see agitation when forgiveness is brought up.
5. Lead in repentance and renunciation. Once a door is identified, stop and lead the person through closing it. This may involve prayer of repentance, forgiveness, renouncing lies, or breaking covenants.

Closing Thoughts

Open doors are the enemy's access points. If you want deliverance to be lasting, you must help people identify, repent, and close those doors. This is where wisdom and patience come in.

Don't be discouraged if closing doors feels slow or messy. It is worth it. Every time a person repents, forgives, or renounces a lie, a chain falls off. Every time a covenant is broken, an inheritance of freedom is released.

Remember: casting out demons is not enough. You must also close the doors. That's how people stay free. That's how the enemy loses his grip. And that's how the Kingdom of God advances—one closed door at a time.

Reflection Questions

1. This chapter shows that not all open doors come from rebellion—some come from trauma, some from lies, and some from generational patterns. Looking at your own life or people you've ministered to, which types of open doors tend to be the most hidden or hardest to identify? Why do you think some doors stay concealed until the Holy Spirit exposes them?

2. Deliverance is lasting only when the legal doors are closed. How have you seen repentance, forgiveness, or renouncing lies shift the atmosphere in a person's soul or deliverance session? Which of these three—repentance, forgiveness, or renunciation—do you personally find hardest to lead people through, and why?

3. The chapter teaches the value of preparation ("Set Free process") but also the need for flexibility when manifestations happen unexpectedly. How do you discern when to slow down and walk someone through doors one by one, versus when to move quickly and respond in the moment? What risks arise when ministers handle "immediate deliverance moments" without discernment or wisdom?

5

MANIFESTATIONS AND SYMPTOMS OF DEMONIC INFLUENCE

WHEN WE STEP INTO DELIVERANCE MINISTRY, ONE OF THE FIRST things we encounter is the reality that demons resist leaving. They don't like being exposed, and they don't like losing ground. Because of this, people often experience manifestations—outward signs of demonic activity—during ministry.

It is essential for a deliverance minister to understand what manifestations are, how to discern them, and how to respond without fear or sensationalism. Manifestations are not proof of power, and they are not the goal of deliverance. They are simply symptoms of an unseen battle. If you can learn to discern manifestations for what they are, you will minister with confidence, clarity, and calmness.

How Demons Operate in Body, Mind, and Emotions

To understand manifestations, we must first understand how demons operate. Demons are disembodied spirits, and they seek expression through human bodies. Jesus said in Matthew 12:43–44 that when an unclean spirit goes out of a person, it seeks rest and finds none, then says, "I will return to my house from which I came." They see people's bodies as their "house" or dwelling place.

In the body:

Demons often attach to physical areas and express themselves through symptoms. They may cause pain, tightness, sickness, or unusual strength. For example, a spirit of infirmity may cause chronic pain or weakness. A spirit of fear may cause shortness of breath or shaking.

In the mind:

Demons attack through intrusive thoughts, confusion, torment, or lies. They whisper accusations like, "You'll never be free," or "God doesn't love you." They use mental pressure to keep people bound.

In the emotions:

Demons stir extreme feelings—sudden rage, despair, panic, or shame. While not every emotion is demonic, extreme or uncontrollable emotions can reveal a spirit at work.

In deliverance ministry, these operations often surface when you pray. As the Spirit confronts the demonic, what was hidden becomes exposed. That's when manifestations occur.

Common Signs During Ministry

Here are some of the most common manifestations you may encounter:

- Shaking or trembling. The person may shake uncontrollably as the spirit reacts to the presence of God.
- Coughing, yawning, or vomiting. Demons often exit through the breath, and physical release can happen this way.
- Eyes rolling or glaring. Demons sometimes look out through the eyes, showing defiance.
- Unusual strength. Just as in the Gospels, some demons manifest with bursts of strength. This is why safety and helpers are important.
- Sudden pain or pressure. The person may grab their head, chest, or stomach as the spirit resists leaving.
- Vocal changes. The person may growl, scream, or speak in a voice not their own. At times, the demon may even attempt to dialogue.
- Laughter or mocking. Some spirits manifest with mocking laughter to distract or intimidate.
- Tears or extreme emotions. The person may suddenly cry, scream, or express overwhelming anger.
- Restlessness or trying to flee. The person may attempt to get up and leave, as the spirit resists exposure.

It is important to note: manifestations vary. Some are dramatic, others are subtle. Sometimes a person will barely move, but afterward they testify, "I felt something leave me." Never judge deliverance by outward display alone.

Manifestation vs. Deliverance — Discerning the Difference

One of the greatest mistakes in this ministry is confusing manifestation with deliverance. Just because a demon screams, shakes, or thrashes does not mean it has left. Manifestation is resistance. Deliverance is departure.

Think of it like this: manifestation is the demon throwing a tantrum. Deliverance is the demon being escorted out. If you don't discern the difference, you may celebrate too early.

Here are some ways to discern if a manifestation is just noise or if actual deliverance has happened:

- Manifestation continues without relief. If the person is thrashing, coughing, or screaming but afterward still feels tormented, the spirit likely has not left.
- Sudden peace and calm. True deliverance is followed by peace. The person's countenance shifts, their eyes clear, and their body rests.
- Testimony of release. Often the person will say, "It's gone. I feel lighter. I feel free." Manifestation does not bring peace; deliverance does.

As ministers, our job is not to chase manifestations but to command deliverance. We don't get distracted by the show; we press through until the spirit leaves and freedom comes.

Responding Without Fear

When manifestations happen, some ministers panic. The person falls to the ground, screams, or contorts, and the minister freezes. Fear paralyzes. But here is the truth: demons are defeated. Jesus disarmed principalities and powers at the cross (Colossians 2:15). They have no authority over you.

Fear has no place in deliverance. Demons may try to intimidate, but remember—they are liars. They may roar like a lion, but only Jesus is the Lion of Judah. When fear rises, silence it with the Word. Declare, "Greater is He who is in me than he who is in the world" (1 John 4:4).

You do not need to raise your voice or strive. Authority is not about volume. It is about confidence in Christ. Speak firmly, command clearly, and trust that the Spirit is backing you up.

Responding Without Sensationalism

You don't have to make deliverance a big show. Some ministries do emphasize dramatic manifestations, and in certain nations or houses that's part of the culture. As a deliverance minister, you must understand that culture and respect the way your leader stewards it.

In the house I lead, at SOZO Church, we don't try to seek manifestations or make them the center of attention. Our focus is always Jesus and the freedom He brings. But I also recognize that in different parts of the world—like in Africa where I minister often—culture may look different, and that is okay. What matters is that you minister in a way that honors your leader and carries the spirit, heart, and culture of the house you serve in.

Guarding Atmosphere

As a deliverance minister, you are also a steward of atmosphere. Manifestations can quickly create fear or distraction in a room. Part of your role is to guard the atmosphere so that the focus stays on Jesus.

When manifestations happen in a service, there are

different ways leaders handle it. In some houses, the team may gently move the person to a side room so the service can continue without distraction. That's one option, and at times it may be best.

But in other houses, manifestations are allowed to happen publicly because it produces an atmosphere of hunger and boldness. People see freedom happening, and it stirs faith in their own hearts. They think, "If God can set them free, maybe He can set me free too." That's powerful.

In the culture of SOZO Church, when someone manifests in a service, we deliver them right there in front of everyone. But we do it with authority and order so it doesn't become a sideshow. The goal is not distraction, but demonstration. The whole room gets to witness freedom, and often it opens the door for many others to come forward for prayer.

As I teach you in this manual, I want you to understand both perspectives. Whether your leader directs you to move someone aside or to minister deliverance openly, your role is to serve the vision of the house. If you've been entrusted with deliverance ministry, then carry the heart and culture of your leader as you minister. That will keep you in unity and make sure the fruit of deliverance strengthens the whole church family.

Stories from Ministry

I've had countless sessions where demons manifested loudly—yelling, shaking, or thrashing. But I've also had many sessions where deliverance was quiet. Sometimes the only sign was a deep sigh, tears, or the person saying, "It's gone." Both are deliverance. Both are victory.

I remember once ministering to someone tormented by fear. As I commanded the spirit to leave, their body shook, and their hands clenched. For several minutes, there was clear manifestation. But then suddenly, they collapsed into peace, their face softened, and they whispered, "I feel free." That was deliverance.

Another time, a woman came for prayer for anxiety. As we prayed, she didn't shake or scream. She simply exhaled, tears ran down her face, and she said, "The weight is gone." That too was deliverance.

Never judge the power of God by how loud the demon leaves. The true test is the fruit of peace, joy, and freedom in the person's life.

Manifestations are real, but they are not the measure of deliverance. They are simply the enemy's reaction to being exposed and evicted. As ministers, we must discern the difference between manifestation and true freedom, and we must respond with calmness, authority, and love.

Do not fear manifestations, and do not glorify them. Keep your eyes on Jesus. He is the Deliverer. Your role is to stand in His authority, close the doors, command the spirits, and lead people into the peace of His presence.

When you keep this perspective, manifestations will not shake you. You will recognize them for what they are—symptoms of an enemy that has already been defeated.

Reflection Questions

1. THIS CHAPTER TEACHES THAT MANIFESTATIONS ARE NOT PROOF of freedom, but signs of resistance. How do you personally discern when a manifestation is simply noise versus when true deliverance has actually taken place? What signs of *peace, rest,* or *shifted countenance* do you look for as evidence of real freedom?

2. THINK ABOUT HOW YOU NATURALLY RESPOND TO DRAMATIC moments—crisis, conflict, or spiritual intensity. Do you tend more toward fear, freezing up, or toward excitement and intensity? How might those tendencies show up in deliverance ministry, and what steps can you take to cultivate calm, grounded, Christ-centered authority regardless of what manifests?

3. THIS CHAPTER HIGHLIGHTS THAT DIFFERENT CHURCHES HANDLE manifestations differently—some take people to a side room, while others (like SOZO Church) minister publicly. Why is honoring the culture of your house and the leadership you serve under vital in deliverance ministry? How does unity with your leaders and atmosphere stewardship shape the fruit of deliverance in a congregation?

6

THE MINISTRY FLOW — FROM START TO FINISH

DELIVERANCE MINISTRY IS NOT MEANT TO BE CHAOTIC OR confusing. When you understand the flow, you'll see that it is actually very simple: prepare, discern, close the doors, command the spirits to leave, and then help the person receive healing, freedom, and peace.

This chapter will walk you step by step through a typical deliverance session. Every situation is different, and you must always stay sensitive to the Holy Spirit, but having a clear framework gives you confidence and helps the person feel safe as they walk through the process.

Preparing Yourself

Before you ever step into ministry with someone else, you must prepare yourself.

- Prayer. Take time to pray in the Spirit before the session. Ask the Lord to cover you with His presence, to sharpen your discernment, and to surround you with angels.

- Holiness. Make sure your own heart is clean. Repent of anything the Spirit brings to mind. Keep your armor strong.
- Authority. Remind yourself of your position in Christ. You are seated with Him in heavenly places (Ephesians 2:6). You are not going into the session timidly but with the authority of Jesus.
- Team. Make sure you have at least one trusted helper with you. Clarify roles before you begin.

When you step into the room, you want to be spiritually sharp, emotionally steady, and fully aware that it is Christ in you who does the work.

Preparing the Recipient

Preparation also matters for the person receiving ministry. Help them understand what is about to happen.

- Explain deliverance. In simple terms, tell them, "We are going to pray together and ask Jesus to set you free from anything that has had a grip on your life. Some things may come up, but don't be afraid— Jesus is here to bring freedom."
- Set expectations. Let them know that manifestations are possible, but the goal is peace and freedom. Tell them, "You may feel pressure, heat, shaking, or even nothing at all. That's okay. What matters is that you are free when we're finished."
- Build faith. Encourage them with Scripture. Remind them of Luke 10:19: "*Behold, I give you authority... over*

all the power of the enemy, and nothing shall by any means hurt you."

A prepared recipient is less likely to be fearful or confused when things begin to happen.

Interview and Assessment

Before jumping into prayer, take a few minutes to ask questions. This isn't an interrogation—it's a pastoral conversation to help identify open doors and strongholds.

Some questions you might ask:

- "When did you first begin experiencing these struggles?"
- "Have you ever been involved in the occult, witchcraft, or New Age practices?"
- "Are there areas of unforgiveness in your life?"
- "Do you struggle with recurring sin or addictive patterns?"
- "Does your family have a history of certain struggles, like addiction, abuse, or sickness?"

As you listen, watch for patterns. Pay attention to the Spirit's nudges. Sometimes the answers reveal clear open doors. Other times, the Spirit will give you impressions beyond what the person says.

Don't overcomplicate this step. You're not trying to gather every detail. You're simply asking enough to know where to start.

Leading Repentance and Renunciation

The foundation of deliverance is closing doors through repentance and renunciation. Demons cling to legal rights, but when the blood of Jesus is applied, those rights are canceled.

Lead the person in simple prayers like:

- "Lord, I repent for partnering with fear. I renounce every agreement I've made with fear, and I choose to trust You."
- "I forgive [name] for what they did to me. I release them to You, and I ask You to heal my heart."
- "I break every soul tie with [name] from sexual sin. I declare that I am one with Christ alone."
- "I renounce every generational curse of addiction in my family line. I belong to Jesus, and His blood is my covenant."

These prayers do not have to be complicated. They must be heartfelt. When repentance and renunciation happen, the enemy's grip is broken.

Practical Deliverance Language (Pact Commands)

Once doors are closed, it is time to directly confront the spirits. This is where authority and clarity matter. Your words are not magic formulas, but they carry power when spoken in Jesus' name.

Here are examples of clear, authoritative commands:

- "I command the spirit of anxiety and all of its kingdom to leave now in Jesus' name."
- "I bind the spirit of infirmity and every spirit under its authority. I command you to go to the pit right now."

- "I break every generational curse of witchcraft, and I command every spirit connected to it to leave in Jesus' name."
- "I bind the spirit of lust and every spirit under its kingdom. I command you to go now to the place the Lord Jesus sends you."

Notice the structure:

1. Identify the spirit. (Anxiety, infirmity, lust, fear, etc.)
2. Bind the spirit and its kingdom. (Demons rarely work alone; they cluster.)
3. Command it to leave in Jesus' name. (Always in His authority, never your own.)

Be firm, clear, and authoritative. You don't need to shout, but you must speak with conviction. Demons respond to authority, not volume.

Handling Resistance

Sometimes spirits resist leaving. That's when you press in with authority. You might say:

- "I command you to stand up and look me in the eyes."
- "By the throne of God, speak the truth—what is your name and your legal right?"
- "Holy Spirit, release judgment on this spirit until it obeys."

Once the spirit is identified and the legal right is addressed (through repentance or forgiveness), its power is broken, and you command it to leave.

Always bring the person back into the process. For example, if the spirit reveals unforgiveness, pause and lead the person in forgiving. Once they forgive, return to commanding the spirit to go. This keeps the person engaged and closes the door permanently.

Watching for Release

As you minister, watch for signs that the spirit has left:

- The person exhales deeply, coughs, or vomits.
- Their body relaxes suddenly.
- Their eyes clear and peace fills their countenance.
- They testify, "I feel lighter. It's gone."

But be careful here—sometimes that moment of release only means one strongman spirit has left. Often there are others hiding behind it. For this reason, I always double-check. If the person has been fully manifesting, I will say something like:

- "I command the next highest-ranking spirit in this body to come up behind you."
- "I command you to come up, look me in the eyes, and declare who you are and what you're doing here."

When you do this, if there are more spirits, they will begin to come one after another. It becomes a process of walking the person through repentance for each legal right, then casting the spirit out, until no more rise up.

Sometimes the first sign of release is true completion— peace, rest, and freedom. Other times, it's only the beginning of a sequence. That's why wisdom says: don't stop too soon, and don't assume the work is finished until you've tested it.

Transitioning Into Healing, Freedom, and Peace

Deliverance does not end with casting demons out. It ends with filling the person with the presence of God.

Always pray for the Holy Spirit to come and fill every place that was emptied. Lay hands and declare:

- "Holy Spirit, fill every part of their heart, soul, and body with Your presence."
- "Lord, restore joy where there was sorrow, peace where there was fear, and strength where there was weakness."
- "I bless you to walk in freedom, to live in holiness, and to know your identity in Christ."

This transition is vital. Without it, people may feel empty or uncertain. With it, they walk away not only free from demons but also filled with the Spirit and empowered to live differently.

Keeping It Simple

The ministry flow of deliverance is not complicated. Don't let the enemy trick you into overthinking. Here is the process in its simplest form:

1. Prepare yourself.
2. Prepare the recipient.
3. Ask a few questions to discern open doors.
4. Lead in repentance and renunciation.
5. Command the spirits to leave in Jesus' name.

6. Watch for release—and check for more if necessary.

7. Pray for the Holy Spirit to fill and seal the work.

Stay flexible. Sometimes you'll move quickly through steps. Sometimes you'll pause on one. But if you keep this simple flow in mind, you'll always have a clear path forward.

A Final Word

Deliverance ministry is not about technique—it's about Jesus. But having a clear flow gives you confidence and helps the person receiving ministry feel safe and cared for.

Always remember: your authority is in His name, your confidence is in His finished work, and your goal is not just casting demons out but seeing people healed, free, and at peace.

When you minister this way—with preparation, repentance, clear commands, wisdom to press through layers, and Spirit-filled aftercare—you will see captives set free and lives transformed, not just for a moment but for eternity.

Reflection Questions

1. This chapter emphasizes that deliverance starts long before commanding spirits—it begins with preparing your heart, your team, and your spiritual posture. Which part of personal preparation (prayer, holiness, identity, or team unity) do you believe is the most crucial for you right now, and why? How might neglecting that area impact a deliverance session?

2. Deliverance is effective only when doors are closed through repentance and renunciation. Why do you think repentance is often the most resisted step for people? How have you seen—or can you imagine—repentance and renunciation shift the entire direction or atmosphere of a session?

3. During a session, ministers must recognize whether they are dealing with one spirit, multiple layers, or simply manifestations. What indicators help you discern when to press for "the next spirit," when to pause for more repentance, and when to move into healing and infilling? How can a minister avoid both rushing the process *and* dragging it on unnecessarily?

7

THE INTEGRATION OF INNER HEALING AND DELIVERANCE

DELIVERANCE AND INNER HEALING ARE NOT COMPETING ministries—they are two sides of the same coin. If deliverance is about evicting unwanted squatters, inner healing is about repairing the house so they don't come back. One confronts the demonic; the other restores the soul. When these ministries flow together, freedom is not only gained but kept.

I want to keep this chapter surface-level, because I have an entire training manual dedicated to inner healing. But because inner healing and deliverance are so deeply connected, every deliverance minister needs at least a working knowledge of how they integrate. If you miss this, you may cast out demons only to see them return, because the wounds that gave them access were never addressed.

Why Wounds Attract Spirits

Broken places in the soul act like open doors. Trauma, abuse, betrayal, rejection, and deep pain create unhealed wounds. Demons are opportunists—they look for those wounds to exploit.

For example:

- A child abandoned by a parent may grow up with a wound of rejection. That wound becomes an open door for spirits of fear, insecurity, or loneliness.
- A teenager abused may internalize the lie, "I am worthless." That lie becomes an open door for spirits of shame and self-hatred.
- Someone betrayed in marriage may make an inner vow, "I'll never trust again." That vow becomes an open door for control, bitterness, or isolation.

The wound itself is not the demon—but it becomes a landing strip. Demons attach themselves to the pain, the lie, or the vow, and use it to gain access. That's why inner healing matters. If you only cast out the demon but never bring Jesus into the wound, the door remains open, and the enemy will try to return.

The Role of Inner Healing

Inner healing is the ministry of Jesus coming into the broken places of a person's heart to bring truth, love, and restoration. It is not counseling in the natural sense—it is Spirit-led and supernatural.

The Bible says Jesus came "to heal the brokenhearted" (Luke 4:18). This is not just poetic language. It is literal. He heals the inner wounds of the heart. Inner healing invites Jesus into those memories, moments, and lies so He can speak His truth and restore wholeness.

At its simplest, inner healing involves:

1. Identifying a wound, lie, or painful memory.
2. Inviting Jesus into that place in prayer.
3. Allowing Him to reveal His presence, truth, or perspective.
4. Replacing the lie with His truth.
5. Walking the person into forgiveness where needed.

When that happens, the wound closes, the lie is broken, and the demon loses its landing strip. Deliverance becomes easier, faster, and more lasting.

A Surface-Level Explanation of the Process

Again, I won't go in-depth here—that's what my Inner Healing Manual is for. But let me give you a surface-level overview so you can see how deliverance and inner healing weave together.

1. Inviting Jesus Into Memories

Often, the Holy Spirit will highlight a memory where pain entered. You don't need every detail—just enough for the person to identify the moment. Lead them in a simple prayer:

- "Jesus, I invite You into this memory. Where were You? What do You want me to know?"

The Spirit will often give them an image, word, or sense of His presence that rewrites how they see that event.

2. Breaking Lies

Wounds always carry lies. The enemy whispers things like: "You're alone. You're worthless. You're unlovable." Once the person identifies the lie, lead them to renounce it and declare truth.

- "I renounce the lie that I am worthless. I declare the truth that I am loved, chosen, and valuable in Christ."

3. Forgiveness

Healing almost always requires forgiveness. Sometimes it's forgiving others, sometimes forgiving themselves, and sometimes releasing anger toward God. Lead them gently:

- "Lord, I choose to forgive [name] for what they did. I release them from my judgment and give them to You."

Forgiveness closes one of the strongest doors demons use.

4. Releasing Inner Vows

When pain leads to vows like "I'll never trust again" or "I'll never cry", those must be broken. Lead the person to say:

- "I break the vow that I will never trust. I choose to trust Jesus and walk in freedom."

5. Inviting Healing

Finally, pray blessing:

"Holy Spirit, fill this place with Your peace. Restore joy where there was sorrow. Seal this memory with Your truth."

This simple process brings deep healing, even in just a few minutes.

Recognizing When to Shift to Inner Healing

As a deliverance minister, you must learn to discern when a manifestation is demonic resistance and when it is a wounded part of the soul surfacing. Here are five examples of manifestations that often indicate it's time to shift from deliverance into inner healing:

1. Tears of Sadness, Not Torment.
2. If a person has been manifesting with anger or growling, and suddenly they begin to cry—not in fear or torment, but with deep sadness—this often means a soul wound has surfaced. At this point, I usually pause deliverance and invite Jesus into the place of pain.
3. Childlike Behavior.
4. Sometimes a person will suddenly begin to act or sound like a child. This may indicate a wounded or fragmented part of the soul is surfacing, often tied to childhood trauma. Rather than commanding a demon, pause and ask Jesus to minister to that childlike part.
5. Sudden Overwhelming Shame.
6. If someone suddenly covers their face, hides, or expresses deep feelings of worthlessness, this may be a wound of shame rather than direct demonic manifestation. Lead them in renouncing lies and receiving the truth of God's love.
7. Frozen or Dissociative State.
8. At times, a person may go still and seem "far away," as if they've disconnected. This is often dissociation

tied to trauma. In this case, the focus should shift to gently grounding them and inviting Jesus into the memory.

9. Flashbacks or Vivid Memories.
10. If, during deliverance, a person suddenly recalls or describes a past event with vivid emotion, that is usually a soul wound surfacing. Help them process it with Jesus rather than pushing deliverance commands at the moment.

These shifts don't mean the person doesn't need deliverance—they usually need both. But when the wound comes to the surface, deal with it first. Once the wound is healed, the demons lose their ground and deliverance becomes much easier.

How Inner Healing Helps Deliverance

When inner healing happens, deliverance flows naturally. Demons cling to wounds, lies, and unforgiveness. Once those things are healed, the spirits lose their legal rights.

For example, if a demon of rejection is exposed, it usually clings to a wound of abandonment. If you try to cast it out without addressing the wound, it may resist. But if you invite Jesus into the wound, break the lie, and lead the person to forgive, the demon loses its ground. Then when you command it to go, it leaves easily.

This is why I often tell ministers: if deliverance feels stuck, pause and switch to inner healing. Ask the Holy Spirit to show the root wound. Address it with the person. Then return to deliverance. You'll often see immediate breakthrough.

The Balance of Simplicity and Depth

One caution here: don't overcomplicate inner healing in a deliverance session. Sometimes a quick moment of forgiveness or breaking a lie is enough. Other times, the person needs a full session of inner healing ministry, not just a few minutes.

As a deliverance minister, learn to recognize when to pause briefly for healing and when to refer someone for a longer, dedicated inner healing session. Not everything can or should be done in one sitting. Freedom is a process.

Referral to Full Training

Because inner healing is such a deep and vital ministry, I've written a full Inner Healing Manual that walks through these processes in detail. That manual covers topics like trauma, dissociation, protector parts, ritual abuse, and complex wounds —all at a depth this book cannot provide.

For the sake of this manual, remember this: inner healing and deliverance belong together. You cannot separate them if you want lasting fruit. But for in-depth training and a full equipping, see my Inner Healing Manual.

Closing Thoughts

Deliverance is about casting out demons. Inner healing is about healing the broken places of the heart. One without the other is incomplete. But when they work together, the enemy is driven out and the soul is restored.

You don't need to master every detail of inner healing to be effective in deliverance, but you do need to understand how they integrate. Pay attention to wounds. Invite Jesus into memories. Break lies. Lead in forgiveness. Close the doors. Then cast out the spirits.

That simple integration will make your ministry far more effective. And when needed, refer people to a deeper process of inner healing so they can walk in full wholeness.

Remember: freedom is not just the absence of demons. Freedom is the presence of Jesus filling every wound, lie, and memory with His love and truth. That's the goal of inner healing and deliverance together.

Reflection Questions

1. THIS CHAPTER TEACHES THAT MANY DEMONIC STRONGHOLDS are attached to unhealed wounds, lies, inner vows, or trauma. Why do you think it is often easier for people to seek "quick deliverance" than to allow Jesus to touch deep places of pain? What does this reveal about the human heart—and how does it shape the way you should minister?

2. AS A MINISTER, HOW DO YOU PERSONALLY DISCERN WHETHER A manifestation is demonic resistance or a wounded part of the soul surfacing (such as childlike behavior, deep sadness, dissociation, or shame)? What indicators would cause you to pause deliverance commands and shift into inner healing instead?

3. THIS CHAPTER WARNS AGAINST OVERCOMPLICATING INNER healing during deliverance while also cautioning not to ignore deep wounds that require dedicated ministry. How do you determine what can be handled briefly in a deliverance session versus what requires a full inner healing appointment? What wisdom or boundaries do you need in place to discern the difference?

8

WHEN SPIRITS MANIFEST AND SPEAK

MOST OF THE TIME IN DELIVERANCE, DEMONS LEAVE QUIETLY. YOU command them to go in Jesus' name, the person exhales, peace comes, and that's it. But there are times when spirits resist. They manifest loudly, speak through the person, or even try to intimidate.

If you're going to be an effective deliverance minister, you need to know what to do in those moments. You don't need to fear them. You don't need to make a spectacle. But you do need to know how to take authority, establish dominance, and bring the person into lasting freedom.

When a Spirit Resists

Sometimes, when you command a demon to leave, it will scream, growl, or shout something like, "No! They're mine!" This is intimidation. Demons know they are defeated, but they try to bluff their way into staying.

When this happens, don't back down. Don't argue. Don't let

it rattle you. Simply take authority. A resisting spirit is like a cornered animal—it thrashes, but it has already lost.

Commands to Establish Authority

When a spirit manifests and speaks, I give clear, authoritative commands to bring it under submission. Examples include:

- "I command you to stand up and look me in the eyes."
- "I command you, in the name of Jesus, to speak your name and your legal right in this body."

When the spirit obeys these commands, it is a sign that the authority of Christ is working. Demons hate being exposed, but exposure strips their power. Once they are identified, their grip begins to break.

If the Spirit Refuses

Sometimes the demon refuses to answer or lies. In that case, I press further with language like:

- "Before the throne of God, I command you to speak the truth—what is your name and what is your legal right?"
- "Holy Spirit, I ask You right now to release judgment on this spirit until it obeys."

At this point, most spirits yield. They know they are subject to the authority of Christ and cannot resist forever. By invoking the throne of God and the presence of the Holy Spirit, you remind the demon of the authority structure it is under.

Why Knowing the Name Helps

It is not always necessary to know a demon's name. Jesus cast out many without asking. But when a spirit manifests and resists, learning its name can help.

Knowing the name establishes dominance. It's like calling a dog by name—it listens better. Names often reveal function. For example, if the spirit says, "I am infirmity," you immediately know its assignment and can target the open door.

Don't get caught up in chasing names, but when the spirit is resisting and the Holy Spirit leads, use this strategy. It helps clarify what you're dealing with and strips away deception.

Leading the Person Into Repentance

Once a spirit reveals its legal right, the next step is not to argue with the demon but to lead the person into repentance. For example:

- If the spirit says, "Unforgiveness toward their mother," pause. Bring the person back up and gently lead them:

- "Do you choose to forgive your mother right now?" •Help them pray: "Lord, I forgive my mother for [specific offense]. I release her into Your hands."

- If the spirit says, "Generational covenant," then lead the person:

- "Lord, I renounce every generational curse of [name it]. I declare that I am under the blood of Jesus."

- If the spirit says, "Pornography," then lead the person in repentance:

- "Lord, I repent for opening the door through pornography. I renounce lust, and I choose purity."

Once the person repents and renounces, the demon's legal right is broken. It has no more permission to stay. At that point, you return to commanding it to leave.

Binding the Spirit to Renounce Itself

One of the most effective strategies in these moments is to bind the spirit and command it to declare its own defeat. I often say something like:

"I bind you in the name of Jesus. Repeat after me: 'I, [spirit's name], bind myself to all my kingdom, and me and all my kingdom go to the pit now.'"

Forcing the spirit to confess its own destruction is powerful. It's like making the enemy sign its own eviction notice. Once it has said the words, you then command:

"Now go, in the name of Jesus, to the pit."

And it will leave.

Dealing With Multiple Spirits

Often, when one spirit is cast out, there are others behind it. That's why after one leaves, I will say:

"I command the next highest-ranking spirit in this body to come up

behind you. Manifest now, look me in the eyes, and declare your name and your legal right."

In many cases, the spirits will come one after another. Each time, you lead the person in repentance for the legal right, then command the spirit to bind itself and its kingdom and go to the pit. This may happen multiple times in one session.

Be patient. Freedom often comes layer by layer. Don't be discouraged if there are many. Each one leaving is another step into wholeness.

Staying in Control

Remember: you are never at the mercy of the demon. You carry authority in Christ. You are the one in control.

- If the demon tries to thrash, command it: "Stand still."
- If it tries to hide, command it: "Come up and manifest."
- If it tries to speak lies, command it: "By the throne of God, speak truth only."

You set the tone. You keep the order. The Holy Spirit backs your words.

The Balance of Humility and Authority

A word of caution: don't let moments like these feed your pride. It is powerful when demons obey, but remember why they obey—it's because of Christ in you, not you.

Luke 10:20 reminds us, *"Nevertheless do not rejoice in this, that the spirits are subject to you, but rather rejoice because your names are written in heaven."* Celebrate the freedom of the person and the grace of God, not your own authority.

At the same time, don't be timid. You don't need to apologize to demons. You don't need to hesitate. Speak boldly. Carry yourself with authority. Humility is knowing it's Him in you, not weakness pretending you don't carry power.

When spirits manifest and speak, don't panic and don't glorify the drama. Stay calm, stay in authority, and stay Spirit-led.

- Command them to submit.
- Require them to speak truth.
- Lead the person in repentance for legal rights.
- Bind the spirit to renounce itself and its kingdom.
- Cast it out in the name of Jesus.
- Call up the next one until there are no more.

This process may sound intense, but it is actually very simple when you are walking in the authority of Christ. Remember: the same Jesus who silenced demons in the synagogue lives in you. His authority is your authority. His Spirit is your strength.

You are not just a spectator in these moments—you are a vessel of the Deliverer. When you stand firm, lives will be changed, bondages will be broken, and the enemy will flee, one spirit at a time.

Reflection Questions

1. WHEN A DEMON RESISTS—MANIFESTING LOUDLY, LYING, OR refusing commands—what does your reaction reveal about your internal view of spiritual authority? Do you naturally shrink back, get tense, or rise in confidence? Why is maintaining calm authority (not fear, not pride) so crucial in these moments?

2. THIS CHAPTER EMPHASIZES THAT RESISTANCE USUALLY REVEALS a deeper legal right. How does leading a person into repentance, forgiveness, or renunciation change the entire dynamic of a deliverance session? Can you think of a scenario (real or hypothetical) where breakthrough required addressing the legal right before the spirit could be cast out?

3. WHEN SPIRITS MANIFEST AND SPEAK, THE TEMPTATION EXISTS either to panic or to treat the moment like a supernatural spectacle. How do you personally guard your heart from both extremes? What practical steps help you remain Spirit-led, people-focused, and centered on Jesus when resistance becomes dramatic?

9

INDIVIDUAL AND CORPORATE DELIVERANCE

DELIVERANCE MINISTRY DOES NOT ALWAYS LOOK THE SAME. Sometimes the Holy Spirit leads you into a one-on-one session in a private setting. Other times, deliverance breaks out in a corporate gathering, at the altar, or even in a revival service. Both are biblical. Both are powerful. And both require discernment and wisdom to steward well.

In this chapter, I want to give you practical guidelines for ministering deliverance both privately and publicly, so that you can guard order, protect safety, and see freedom flow in whatever setting the Spirit chooses.

When Ministry Should Be Private

There are times when deliverance should be handled privately rather than in front of a crowd.

Sensitive Issues

If someone's deliverance is tied to very personal sins,

trauma, or abuse, it may be best to move into a private room or small setting. Not every detail needs to be exposed to the whole church. Protecting dignity is always important.

Prolonged Ministry

Sometimes deliverance takes time. If someone needs extensive repentance, inner healing, or layer-by-layer breakthrough, a private session may be best so you can go at the pace required without disrupting the flow of a service.

Safety Concerns

If someone is manifesting with violent thrashing, unusual strength, or behavior that could harm themselves or others, it is wise to move them to a safe place with trained ministers.

Private deliverance is not "less spiritual." It is often the most loving and effective way to minister freedom in certain circumstances.

Dynamics of Corporate/Altar Deliverance

But there are also times when deliverance should happen publicly. Jesus Himself cast out demons in synagogues and public spaces. In Acts 8, Philip ministered deliverance to crowds in Samaria, and the Bible says, *"with shrieks, impure spirits came out of many"* (Acts 8:7 NIV). Corporate deliverance is biblical and powerful.

Why Public Deliverance Matters

When deliverance happens in a service, it:

- Reveals the reality of the kingdom. People see that Jesus still has authority over demons.
- Stirs hunger and boldness. When people witness freedom, faith rises for their own deliverance.
- Creates testimony. Public deliverance becomes a living demonstration of the gospel.

Guarding the Atmosphere

Public deliverance requires strong leadership. It can either stir faith or create distraction. That's why you must guard the atmosphere. Make sure the focus stays on Jesus, not the demon.

At SOZO Church, when someone manifests at the altar, we deliver them right there in front of everyone. But we train our ministers to carry themselves with calm authority so it doesn't become a spectacle. The room sees freedom, not chaos. And often, many others come forward for prayer because faith has been stirred.

Guarding Order and Safety in Group Settings

When deliverance is happening corporately, here are some principles to keep order and safety:

1. Have a trained team. Don't try to do corporate deliverance alone. Have helpers who know how to pray, assist, and protect.
2. Assign roles. Make sure one person leads, while others cover in prayer, provide physical support if needed, or guard safety.
3. Protect dignity. Cover people with blankets if they fall or thrash. Keep the atmosphere honorable.

4. Maintain authority. Don't let manifestations hijack the service. Keep the room focused on Jesus.
5. Discern timing. Sometimes it's right to pause the whole service and minister freedom corporately. Other times, it's best to continue worship while a team ministers to individuals at the altar.

Remember: order is not the enemy of freedom. Order actually protects freedom. Paul wrote in 1 Corinthians 14:40, "Let all things be done decently and in order." That includes deliverance.

How to Minister Freedom in Public Without Chaos

Corporate deliverance can be powerful without being chaotic. Here are some practical ways to steward it:

Stay Calm and Confident

When a manifestation breaks out, don't panic and don't hype it up. Speak with steady authority. If the leader stays calm, the people will stay calm.

Use Clear Commands

You don't need long prayers in corporate settings. Short, sharp commands are most effective:

- "In the name of Jesus, every spirit of fear, go now."
- "I bind the spirit of witchcraft and command it to leave this person right now."
- "Holy Spirit, fill this place with freedom."

Cover With Worship

Worship teams can play a powerful role in corporate deliverance. As freedom is happening at the altar, let worship continue. It keeps the atmosphere centered on Jesus and prevents distraction.

Keep the Focus on Jesus

After someone is delivered, give space for testimony. But keep the emphasis on what Jesus did, not on the demon. Celebrate freedom, not manifestation.

Train Your People

Teach your church what deliverance is. When the congregation understands, manifestations don't create fear—they create faith. At SOZO, because we've taught on deliverance, our people don't panic when it happens. They celebrate freedom.

Finding the Right Balance

The key is balance. Not every deliverance needs to be public, and not every deliverance needs to be private. Wisdom is knowing which is best in the moment.

- If the Spirit is moving powerfully in a service and people are responding, don't shut it down. Let freedom flow.
- If the manifestation is distracting, dangerous, or deeply personal, move it to a private space.

The goal is always the same: freedom for the person and glory to Jesus. Whether in private or public, if those two things are accomplished, you've done it well.

Deliverance belongs in both the private room and the public altar. Jesus ministered in both contexts, and so should we. The key is wisdom, discernment, and a commitment to protect both the individual and the atmosphere.

When you know when to go private and when to stay public, when to guard dignity and when to stir faith, you will see deliverance ministry flourish in every setting.

Remember: deliverance is not about chasing manifestations —it's about setting captives free. Whether in the quiet of a counseling room or in the midst of a revival altar, the same Jesus delivers. And when He does, the whole house is strengthened, and the kingdom of God advances.

Reflection Questions

1. THIS CHAPTER TEACHES THAT DELIVERANCE IS POWERFUL IN both private sessions and corporate settings, but the setting must match the situation. How do you personally discern when someone's deliverance needs the privacy of a room versus the atmosphere of a public altar? What indicators or red flags guide your decision?

2. PUBLIC DELIVERANCE CAN STIR FAITH, REVEAL JESUS' authority, and strengthen the whole house—but it can also risk embarrassment or distraction if mishandled. How do you balance protecting the dignity of the individual while allowing the Spirit to move powerfully in a corporate setting? What does that look like practically in your ministry context?

3. THIS CHAPTER EMPHASIZES THAT ORDER IS NOT THE ENEMY OF freedom—it protects it. In your view, what are the most important roles or strategies for guarding the atmosphere during a corporate deliverance moment? How does a calm, trained team help prevent chaos and keep the focus on Jesus?

10

THE WORD OF GOD AS A WEAPON

DELIVERANCE IS NOT JUST ABOUT CASTING OUT DEMONS—IT'S about establishing people in truth so they can stay free. And nothing carries greater authority against the enemy than the Word of God.

When Jesus was tempted in the wilderness, He didn't argue with Satan, wrestle with him, or rely on feelings. He spoke the Word. Every time the enemy attacked, Jesus answered, "It is written" (Matthew 4:4, 7, 10). That pattern wasn't just for Him— it was an example for us. If the Son of God defeated Satan with the Word, we must learn to do the same.

The Word of God is a sword (Ephesians 6:17). It is living and active, sharper than any two-edged blade (Hebrews 4:12). It tears down strongholds, exposes lies, and declares the authority of Christ. If you are going to be effective in deliverance, you must know how to wield the Word of God.

Scriptures for Authority and Warfare

There are many passages you will lean on as a deliverance minister. Let me give you a core arsenal of Scriptures that establish your authority, silence the enemy, and release faith for freedom.

Authority of the Believer

- Luke 10:19 — "Behold, I give you authority to trample on serpents and scorpions, and over all the power of the enemy, and nothing shall by any means hurt you."
- Mark 16:17 — "And these signs will follow those who believe: In My name they will cast out demons."
- Ephesians 2:6 — "And raised us up together, and made us sit together in the heavenly places in Christ Jesus."

These verses remind both you and the person receiving ministry that deliverance is not about striving—it's about standing in Christ's authority.

Power of the Name and Blood of Jesus

- Philippians 2:9–10 — "At the name of Jesus every knee should bow, of those in heaven, and of those on earth, and of those under the earth."
- Revelation 12:11 — "And they overcame him by the blood of the Lamb and by the word of their testimony."

The enemy has no defense against the name of Jesus and the power of His blood.

Weapons of Warfare

- 2 Corinthians 10:4–5 — "For the weapons of our warfare are not carnal but mighty in God for pulling down strongholds, casting down arguments and every high thing that exalts itself against the knowledge of God, bringing every thought into captivity to the obedience of Christ."
- Ephesians 6:10–17 — The full armor of God, including the sword of the Spirit, which is the Word of God.

These remind us that our warfare is not natural but spiritual, and our greatest weapon is the Word.

Freedom and Deliverance

- John 8:36 — "Therefore if the Son makes you free, you shall be free indeed."
- Isaiah 61:1 — "The Spirit of the Lord God is upon Me... to proclaim liberty to the captives, and the opening of the prison to those who are bound."

These declarations release faith that freedom is possible and certain in Christ.

Using the Word During Ministry

When I minister deliverance, I use the Word in several ways:

1. Declaring Truth Over the Person
2. Before I command spirits, I often read or quote Scriptures that establish their identity:

- "You are seated with Christ in heavenly places."

- ◦ "Whom the Son sets free is free indeed."
- ◦ This builds faith in the recipient and sets the tone for authority.

3. Confronting Demons With the Word
4. If a spirit resists, I may quote Scriptures directly:

- "It is written, every knee must bow to the name of Jesus."
  - ◦ "It is written, the Son of God was manifested to destroy the works of the devil" (1 John 3:8).
  - ◦ Demons cannot resist the authority of the Word.

5. Guiding Repentance With the Word
6. When leading someone to forgive, I might reference Matthew 6:14–15: "If you forgive men their trespasses, your heavenly Father will also forgive you." This shows them why forgiveness matters.
7. Sealing Freedom With the Word
8. After deliverance, I declare verses like Romans 8:1: "There is therefore now no condemnation to those who are in Christ Jesus." This shifts them from battle into rest.

Teaching Recipients to Fight With the Word

Deliverance doesn't end with you casting demons out. The person must learn to fight for themselves with the Word of God. If they don't, old patterns may return. Teaching them to wield the Word is one of the most important parts of aftercare.

Here are some keys to help recipients use the Word:

1. Teach Them Their Identity

Many people struggle because they don't know who they are in Christ. Encourage them to memorize Scriptures on identity:

- "I am a new creation in Christ" (2 Corinthians 5:17).
- "I am more than a conqueror through Him who loved me" (Romans 8:37).
- "I am chosen, holy, and dearly loved" (Colossians 3:12).

When lies attack, they must speak truth out loud.

2. Teach Them to Resist Temptation

Show them how Jesus resisted Satan by saying, "It is written." Encourage them to answer temptation with the Word:

- Against fear: "God has not given me a spirit of fear, but of power, love, and a sound mind" (2 Timothy 1:7).
- Against lust: "Blessed are the pure in heart, for they shall see God" (Matthew 5:8).
- Against discouragement: "The joy of the Lord is my strength" (Nehemiah 8:10).

3. Teach Them to Declare Freedom

Encourage them to declare verses daily, like:

- "Whom the Son sets free is free indeed."
- "No weapon formed against me shall prosper" (Isaiah 54:17).
- "Greater is He who is in me than he who is in the world" (1 John 4:4).

Declarations aren't hype—they are alignment with the truth of God's Word.

4. Teach Them to Meditate on the Word

Joshua 1:8 says, "This Book of the Law shall not depart from your mouth, but you shall meditate in it day and night." Meditation means turning the Word over in your heart until it becomes part of you. Encourage people to soak in Scripture daily so it shapes their thinking.

5. Teach Them to Use the Word in Prayer

Show them how to pray Scripture back to God:

- "Lord, You said no weapon formed against me shall prosper—I claim that promise today."
- "Father, You said if I resist the devil, he will flee from me—I stand on that right now."

Praying Scripture strengthens faith and releases power.

The Word of God is your primary weapon in deliverance ministry. Demons fear it. Lies crumble before it. Freedom is sustained through it.

As a deliverance minister, you must not only wield the Word yourself but also equip others to do the same. Cast out the spirits, yes—but also plant the Word. Teach people to declare truth, resist temptation, and establish their identity in Scripture.

Remember: it is not eloquent prayers or forceful personalities that sustain freedom. It is the living Word of God, sharper than any two-edged sword. When you and those you minister to learn to fight with the Word, deliverance will not just be a moment—it will become a lifestyle of victory.

Reflection Questions

1. THIS CHAPTER SHOWS THAT JESUS USED SCRIPTURE—NOT emotions, techniques, or arguments—to defeat Satan. Why do you think many believers still rely more on feelings, experiences, or personalities than on the Word when facing spiritual warfare? What does this reveal about the role of Scripture in sustaining true freedom?

2. HOW DOES DECLARING SCRIPTURE DURING DELIVERANCE— over the person, against the demon, or in guiding repentance— shift the spiritual atmosphere? Can you think of a moment (real or hypothetical) where quoting the right Scripture could expose a lie, silence a demon, or strengthen the recipient's faith?

3. DELIVERANCE DOESN'T LAST IF THE PERSON DOESN'T LEARN TO fight with the Word. Which of the five tools—identity Scriptures, resisting temptation with "It is written," daily declarations, meditation, or praying Scripture—do you think is most critical for someone newly set free? Why? How would you practically teach a new believer to adopt that practice?

11

THE POWER OF THE NAME AND BLOOD OF JESUS

AT THE CENTER OF DELIVERANCE MINISTRY IS NOT OUR STRENGTH, not our wisdom, not even our prayers—it is the authority of the name of Jesus and the power of His blood. These two realities are what every demon fears most. The name of Jesus is the highest authority in heaven and on earth. The blood of Jesus is the eternal covenant that disarmed the enemy forever.

If you are going to be effective in deliverance ministry, you must understand and fully trust in these truths. Demons do not flee because of your personality, your volume, or even your persistence. They flee because the Son of God conquered them at the cross, and His name and His blood enforce that victory every time.

Authority in the Name Above All Names

Philippians 2:9–10 says, "Therefore God also has highly exalted Him and given Him the name which is above every name, that at the name of Jesus every knee should bow, of those in heaven, and of those on earth, and of those under the earth."

Every knee bows at His name. Every demon trembles at His name. Every curse, every bondage, every principality must submit when the name of Jesus is declared with faith.

Not a Formula, But a Person

The power is not in saying the syllables "Jesus" like a magic word. The power is in the person behind the name. When you declare "In the name of Jesus," you are invoking the authority of the risen Lord who crushed the serpent's head.

Acts 19 tells the story of the sons of Sceva who tried to cast out demons by saying, "We adjure you by the Jesus whom Paul preaches." The demons answered, "Jesus I know, and Paul I know, but who are you?" The name of Jesus is not a formula. It only carries authority when it is backed by relationship. When you belong to Him, His name carries His power in your mouth.

Ministering in His Authority

When you command a demon, say:

- "In the name of Jesus Christ, I command you to go."
- "By the authority of Jesus, the Son of God, I bind you and cast you out."

Speak it with confidence. You are not speaking for yourself —you are representing heaven. The demons aren't responding to you; they're responding to Him in you.

Cleansing and Covering Through the Blood

The blood of Jesus is more than a symbol. It is a weapon.

Revelation 12:11 says, "They overcame him by the blood of the Lamb and by the word of their testimony." The blood overcomes the enemy every time.

The Cleansing Power of the Blood

1 John 1:7 declares, "The blood of Jesus Christ His Son cleanses us from all sin." Sin is the legal right demons cling to. But the moment the blood is applied, those rights are canceled. That's why repentance is so powerful in deliverance—it applies the blood to the open doors.

When leading someone through repentance, I often pray:

- "Lord, we thank You for the blood of Jesus that cleanses and cancels every legal right of the enemy. By the blood, this sin is forgiven, and the power of this spirit is broken."

The Covering Power of the Blood

The blood not only cleanses, it covers. Just as the blood of the lamb on the doorposts protected Israel from the destroyer in Exodus 12, the blood of Jesus covers us today. Demons cannot cross the bloodline.

When I pray protection, I often declare:

- "I plead the blood of Jesus over this person's mind, emotions, and body. I declare that the enemy cannot reenter—this house is covered by the blood."

The Covenant Power of the Blood

The blood represents covenant. Through the cross, Jesus made a new covenant with us, one that is eternal and unbreakable. Demons hate the blood because it is the proof that their hold has been permanently broken. They lost their claim the day the blood was shed.

Why Demons Bow to the Cross and Resurrection

Colossians 2:14–15 gives one of the clearest pictures of deliverance:

"Having wiped out the handwriting of requirements that was against us, which was contrary to us. And He has taken it out of the way, having nailed it to the cross. Having disarmed principalities and powers, He made a public spectacle of them, triumphing over them in it."

At the cross, Jesus disarmed the powers of darkness. Every accusation against us was nailed to the cross. Every curse was broken. Every demonic weapon was stripped. And when He rose from the dead, He sealed that victory forever.

The Cross Broke Their Claim

Demons operate through accusation, guilt, and legal rights. But at the cross, every accusation was answered. Every sin was forgiven. The legal rights they once clung to were wiped away.

The Resurrection Proved Their Defeat

Demons not only fear the cross—they fear the empty tomb. The resurrection proved that Jesus is Lord over death, hell, and the grave. When you invoke the cross and resurrection, you are reminding demons that they are eternally defeated.

That's why in deliverance I often say:

- "You have no more power here. The cross of Christ has disarmed you. The blood of Jesus has cleansed this person. The resurrection of Jesus has sealed your defeat. Go now, in the name of Jesus."

Demons bow to that reality every single time.

Using the Name and Blood Together

While the name of Jesus represents His authority, the blood of Jesus represents His victory. Together they are unstoppable.

- In the name of Jesus, you command the demon to leave.
- By the blood of Jesus, you cancel its rights and seal the person's freedom.

This is why you will often hear me pray something like:

- "In the name of Jesus Christ, I command every spirit of fear to leave. And I plead the blood of Jesus over this person's heart and mind, sealing every door."

The name enforces authority. The blood enforces covenant. Together they ensure victory.

Teaching Believers to Stand in the Name and Blood

One of the greatest gifts you can give someone after deliverance is teaching them how to use the name and the blood for themselves.

- Teach them to pray in the name of Jesus. Encourage them to declare His name over temptation, fear, or spiritual attack.
- Teach them to plead the blood. Encourage them to daily declare, "I am cleansed, covered, and protected by the blood of Jesus."
- Teach them to declare victory. Encourage them to speak out loud: "The cross of Christ has broken every curse. The resurrection of Jesus has sealed my freedom."

When they learn to use these truths, they will not only stay free—they will walk boldly in the authority Christ gave them.

Deliverance ministry begins and ends with Jesus. It is His name and His blood that break every chain. You are simply His vessel, His ambassador, His instrument of freedom.

Never forget:

- Demons don't fear your shouting. They fear His name.
- Demons don't bow to your personality. They bow to His blood.
- Demons don't tremble at your strength. They tremble at His cross and resurrection.

As you minister, stay anchored here. Speak His name with confidence. Plead His blood with faith. Declare His cross and resurrection with boldness. When you do, you will see captives set free again and again, not by your power but by the power of the Lamb who was slain and is now risen.

Reflection Questions

1. THIS CHAPTER TEACHES THAT THE POWER OF JESUS' NAME IS not in the sound of the word "Jesus," but in your relationship with Him. What does this reveal about the difference between spiritual authority and religious formulas? How does this challenge the motives or mindset of someone eager to operate in deliverance?

2. WE OFTEN TALK ABOUT "PLEADING THE BLOOD," BUT THIS chapter explains three distinct functions: cleansing sin, covering for protection, and covenant that cancels legal rights. Which of these aspects of the blood do you think believers understand the least—and why do you believe demons fear that specific aspect so deeply?

3. COLOSSIANS 2:14–15 SAYS JESUS ALREADY DISARMED THE powers of darkness at the cross. How does this truth reshape the way deliverance ministers should approach resistance, intimidation, or manifestations? What does it look like to minister *from victory* rather than striving *for victory*?

12

REPENTANCE, RENUNCIATION, AND FORGIVENESS

IF YOU WANT TO SEE LASTING FRUIT IN DELIVERANCE, YOU CANNOT skip over repentance, renunciation, and forgiveness. These are not side issues. They are the very foundation of freedom. Demons don't leave because we yell louder or pray harder. They leave because the blood of Jesus cancels their rights, and those rights are canceled through repentance, renunciation, and forgiveness.

I tell people often: deliverance is not a power encounter; it is a truth encounter. The devil thrives on lies and legal ground. When truth comes in and the blood of Jesus is applied, his grip is broken.

In this chapter, I'll walk you through why repentance, renunciation, and forgiveness matter so much, and I'll give you practical prayers you can use both for yourself and for those you minister to.

Closing Legal Doors Through Repentance

Repentance is the first and most important step in deliverance. Acts 3:19 says, "Repent therefore and be converted, that your sins may be blotted out, so that times of refreshing may come from the presence of the Lord."

Repentance literally means to change your mind and turn around. It is not just saying "sorry." It is aligning yourself with God's truth and turning away from sin.

Why is this important in deliverance? Because sin gives demons legal rights. They claim ownership through rebellion, disobedience, and ungodly agreements. But when someone truly repents, those rights are canceled. The blood of Jesus cleanses, and the door is shut.

Examples of Repentance Prayers

- "Lord, I repent for agreeing with fear. I turn from fear and choose to trust You."
- "Lord, I repent for sexual sin. I renounce lust and pornography, and I choose purity."
- "Lord, I repent for bitterness and anger. I turn from resentment and choose forgiveness."

These prayers don't have to be long. They just have to be sincere. Demons know the difference between empty words and real repentance. When repentance is real, their ground is gone.

Breaking Agreements and Vows Through Renunciation

Repentance closes the door of sin. Renunciation closes the door of agreement. Many times, people are not just bound by what they've done but by what they've said, promised, or aligned themselves with.

Inner Vows

When someone says in their heart, "I'll never trust anyone again" or "I'll always be broken," that becomes a vow. Those vows act like chains in the soul. They give demons ground to enforce lies.

Ungodly Covenants and Practices

If someone has been involved in witchcraft, occult practices, false religions, or unhealthy soul ties, those covenants must be broken through renunciation.

How to Renounce

Renunciation means publicly breaking agreement with darkness and declaring alignment with Christ. The word itself means "to disown" or "to formally declare abandonment."

Examples of Renunciation Prayers

- "I renounce every lie that says I am unlovable. I declare the truth that I am loved by God."
- "I renounce every inner vow that I will never trust again. I break it in Jesus' name and choose to walk in freedom."
- "I renounce every covenant I made with witchcraft, knowingly or unknowingly. I declare I belong to Jesus Christ alone."
- "I renounce every soul tie with [name]. I cut it off in

the name of Jesus and declare my heart belongs to Christ."

Renunciation is like tearing up a contract. Once the contract is destroyed, the enemy has no legal right to enforce it anymore.

Forgiveness as the Central Key to Freedom

If repentance and renunciation close doors, forgiveness is the key that unlocks them. I cannot overstate this: forgiveness is central to deliverance.

Jesus said in Matthew 6:14–15, "For if you forgive men their trespasses, your heavenly Father will also forgive you. But if you do not forgive men their trespasses, neither will your Father forgive your trespasses."

Unforgiveness is one of the strongest footholds demons use. They thrive in bitterness, resentment, and offense. When people refuse to forgive, it's like giving demons a room in their heart with a signed lease.

Why Forgiveness Is Hard

Forgiveness doesn't mean what happened was okay. It doesn't minimize the pain or injustice. It doesn't mean you have to trust the person again. Forgiveness means you release them from your judgment and give them to God.

When people hold onto unforgiveness, they hold onto the chain the enemy is using to bind them. When they forgive, that chain breaks.

Practical Forgiveness Prayers

When leading someone in forgiveness, keep it simple but specific. Have them name the person and the offense. Then lead them in prayer.

Examples:

- "Lord, I forgive my father for abandoning me. I release him into Your hands."
- "Lord, I forgive my friend for betraying me. I let go of the anger and pain, and I release them to You."
- "Lord, I forgive myself for my failures. I receive Your forgiveness and release myself from shame."
- "Lord, I release my anger toward You for not stopping what happened. I trust that You are good and I give this pain to You."

As they pray, listen to the Holy Spirit. Sometimes tears flow. Sometimes anger rises. Sometimes peace floods in immediately. But always, forgiveness opens the way for deliverance.

Bringing It All Together

Repentance, renunciation, and forgiveness often flow together in a deliverance session. It might look like this:

1. Identify the issue. (e.g., fear, lust, rejection)
2. Lead in repentance. "Lord, I repent for opening the door to fear."
3. Lead in renunciation. "I renounce every agreement I made with fear."
4. Lead in forgiveness. "I forgive my father for creating an atmosphere of fear in my home."

5. Apply the blood. Declare, "By the blood of Jesus, this door is closed."

6. Command the spirit. "Spirit of fear, your rights are broken. I command you to leave now in the name of Jesus."

This process is simple, biblical, and effective. It removes the enemy's ground and then evicts him completely.

If you don't deal with repentance, renunciation, and forgiveness, deliverance will be incomplete. You may cast out a spirit, but if the door is still open, it will try to come back.

But when repentance is genuine, renunciation is clear, and forgiveness is released, the enemy loses every foothold. The blood of Jesus covers, the cross cancels, and the Spirit fills. That is how true and lasting freedom comes.

As a minister, don't rush this process. Take time to walk people through it. Sometimes it's the hardest part, but it's also the most powerful. And as you lead people into repentance, renunciation, and forgiveness, you will watch chains fall, hearts heal, and captives go free.

Reflection Questions

1. THE CHAPTER SAYS "DELIVERANCE IS NOT A POWER ENCOUNTER; it is a truth encounter." How does that statement challenge popular ideas about spiritual warfare and deliverance? In your own life, where have you seen that real freedom came not from an intense moment of prayer, but from facing truth and responding with repentance, renunciation, or forgiveness?

2. UNFORGIVENESS, INNER VOWS, AND UNGODLY AGREEMENTS often feel like "self-protection," yet this chapter shows they actually give demons legal ground. Why do people cling so tightly to bitterness or inner vows like "I'll never trust again"? What do you think it practically looks like to help someone move from protecting themselves with those walls to trusting Jesus enough to forgive and renounce them?

3. THIS CHAPTER OUTLINES A SIMPLE FLOW: IDENTIFY THE ISSUE → repent → renounce → forgive → apply the blood → command the spirit to leave. Which step do you personally find the hardest to lead others through, and why? How might skipping or rushing that step affect the outcome of a deliverance session and the person's long-term freedom?

13

BINDING, LOOSING, AND DECLARING FREEDOM

DELIVERANCE MINISTRY IS NOT JUST ABOUT CASTING DEMONS OUT —it is about enforcing the authority of the kingdom of God. One of the most powerful tools Jesus gave us for this is the authority to bind and loose. Along with that, we are called to declare the promises of God and release His destiny over people once the enemy's grip is broken.

This chapter will walk you through what binding and loosing really mean, how to use them to break demonic rights, and how to step into the prophetic declaration that seals freedom and launches people into their calling.

The Biblical Basis for Binding and Loosing

In Matthew 16:19, Jesus told Peter, "I will give you the keys of the kingdom of heaven, and whatever you bind on earth will be bound in heaven, and whatever you loose on earth will be loosed in heaven."

Then in Matthew 18:18, He expanded it to all disciples:

"Assuredly, I say to you, whatever you bind on earth will be bound in heaven, and whatever you loose on earth will be loosed in heaven."

The word bind means to forbid, tie up, or restrict. The word loose means to release, untie, or permit. In deliverance, binding refers to restricting the activity of demons, while loosing refers to releasing God's will, blessing, or destiny.

This is not just nice language—it is the authority of heaven being enforced on earth. Jesus was giving His disciples legal authority to shut down the works of the devil and to open the flow of God's kingdom in people's lives.

Binding Demons

When ministering deliverance, binding is often your first step. Demons often manifest with violence, intimidation, or resistance. Binding restricts their power and brings them under control.

Examples of binding commands include:

- "I bind the spirit of fear and every demon under its authority in the name of Jesus."
- "I bind the strongman of infirmity and forbid your operation in this body."
- "I bind you, spirit of lust, and I cut off your influence over this mind."

Binding is not the same as casting out. Binding is restraining. It's like tying a dog on a leash so it cannot bite. Once bound, the spirit must obey further commands.

Loosing Captives

Loosing is the other side of this authority. Isaiah 61:1 declares, "The Spirit of the Lord God is upon Me... to proclaim liberty to the captives, and the opening of the prison to those who are bound."

When you minister, you are not just binding demons—you are loosing people into freedom. This can look like:

- "I loose you from every chain of fear in the name of Jesus."
- "I loose your mind from torment and confusion."
- "I loose your body from affliction and pain."

Loosing is releasing people from the grip of the enemy and into the freedom of Christ. It is proclaiming liberty with authority, knowing heaven backs your words.

Breaking Demonic Rights

Binding and loosing also tie directly into the breaking of legal rights. When you lead someone through repentance, renunciation, and forgiveness, you are canceling the contracts demons cling to. Once those rights are broken, you declare it with authority:

- "I bind every spirit of bitterness and unforgiveness —your rights are broken by the blood of Jesus."
- "I loose this person into peace, joy, and the love of God."

This is where binding and loosing shift from abstract theology to practical ministry. You are enforcing the legal victory of the cross in real time.

Declaring God's Promises

Deliverance should never stop at eviction. Once demons are cast out and doors are closed, the minister's role is to fill the person with truth and destiny. This is where declaration comes in.

Proverbs 18:21 says, "Death and life are in the power of the tongue, and those who love it will eat its fruit." Your words carry weight. When you declare God's promises, you establish His truth in the person's life.

Examples of declarations you might speak over someone:

- "You are a new creation in Christ—old things have passed away, all things are made new."
- "You are loosed into purity, holiness, and the love of God."
- "I declare over you that no weapon formed against you shall prosper."
- "I declare you will walk in your destiny, free from every chain that once held you."

These declarations are not hype—they are prophecy. You are speaking the Word of God into their spirit and sealing their freedom with truth.

Releasing Destiny

Deliverance is never an end in itself. The goal is not just to remove demons but to release people into their destiny. Once the enemy's grip is broken, you have the privilege of prophetically declaring who they are in Christ.

Here are some examples of how I release destiny over someone after deliverance:

- "I see you stepping into leadership, full of boldness where fear once held you back."
- "I declare over you a spirit of worship and intimacy with God that will break chains in others."
- "I loose you into the ministry of reconciliation—you will heal relationships and restore hope."

The enemy always attacks in the opposite direction of someone's calling. When you see where they were bound, often it reveals what they are called to. Declare that destiny and release them into it.

Putting It All Together

In a typical ministry session, this might look like:

1. Bind the spirit. "I bind you, spirit of lust, and every demon under your authority."
2. Lead the person in repentance and renunciation. "Lord, I repent for agreeing with lust and pornography. I renounce every covenant with impurity."
3. Break the legal right. "By the blood of Jesus, your rights are broken."
4. Command the spirit to go. "Spirit of lust, leave now in the name of Jesus."
5. Loose the person into freedom. "I loose you into purity, holiness, and wholeness."
6. Declare God's promises. "You are a new creation. You are washed and sanctified in Christ."

7. Release destiny. "I declare you will be a man of integrity who leads others into freedom."

This flow ensures that deliverance is not just about casting demons out but about filling, healing, and launching people forward.

Closing Thoughts

Binding and loosing are not complicated concepts. They are simple, powerful keys Jesus gave His church. When you bind demons, they are restricted. When you loose captives, they are freed. And when you declare God's promises, you seal freedom with truth and release people into destiny.

Never forget: the ultimate goal of deliverance is not emptiness—it is fullness. It is not just eviction—it is empowerment. Binding, loosing, and declaring freedom ensure that the person leaves not only free but also filled, affirmed, and released into God's call.

When you step into this authority with humility, faith, and boldness, you will see heaven's reality manifest on earth. Chains will break, lives will change, and the kingdom will advance through your words and your obedience.

Reflection Questions

1. JESUS GAVE THE CHURCH AUTHORITY TO BIND AND LOOSE—restricting demonic activity and releasing freedom. How does this shift your understanding of deliverance from simply "casting out demons" to *enforcing kingdom law*? In what ways have you seen (or can you imagine seeing) binding and loosing change the tone, order, or effectiveness of a deliverance session?

2. THIS CHAPTER TEACHES THAT AFTER DELIVERANCE, MINISTERS must declare truth and release destiny, not merely evict spirits. Why do you think prophetic declaration is so crucial for helping people stay free? How do declarations reshape identity, thought patterns, and atmosphere in ways that simple prayer cannot?

3. DELIVERANCE IS DESCRIBED HERE NOT AS THE FINAL STOP BUT as the doorway into a person's calling. How can a minister practically discern what destiny or calling to declare over someone after deliverance? What safeguards ensure that prophetic releasing is done with accuracy, humility, and alignment with Scripture?

14

BONDAGES OF THE FLESH AND SOUL

DELIVERANCE IS NOT ONLY ABOUT CASTING OUT DEMONS—IT IS about identifying and tearing down the strongholds that give demons access. Many times, people are not primarily bound because of demonic possession but because of entrenched patterns of the flesh or unhealed wounds of the soul. These strongholds become landing strips for the enemy.

If you want to walk in freedom yourself, and if you want to lead others into lasting deliverance, you must learn to discern the bondages of the flesh and the soul. You must know how to expose them, break them, and replace them with the truth of Christ.

Understanding the Nature of Bondage

The Bible describes sin and strongholds as slavery. Jesus said in John 8:34, "Most assuredly, I say to you, whoever commits sin is a slave of sin." Paul wrote in Romans 6:16, "Do you not know that to whom you present yourselves slaves to obey, you are that one's slaves whom you obey?"

Bondages of the flesh and soul are not just bad habits—they are chains. They shape the way people think, feel, and live. They often start small but grow into powerful strongholds that influence identity and destiny.

Demons are opportunists. They look for these bondages and attach themselves to them. That's why breaking free requires more than casting out—it requires identifying and dismantling the root structures in the flesh and soul.

Common Bondages of the Flesh and Soul

Let's look at some of the most common bondages you'll encounter in deliverance ministry.

1. Addictions

Addictions come in many forms: drugs, alcohol, pornography, gambling, even food or technology. At their root, addictions are attempts to fill a void only God can fill. Demons of addiction reinforce the cycle, keeping people enslaved and ashamed.

2. Fear

Fear is one of the most common open doors. It manifests as anxiety, worry, panic attacks, phobias, or obsessive thoughts. Fear often connects to trauma or rejection. Spirits of fear torment the mind and paralyze action.

3. Anger

Uncontrolled anger, rage, and bitterness are major strongholds. These often tie to wounds of betrayal or injustice. When unresolved, anger opens the door for spirits of wrath and violence.

4. Rejection

Rejection is a deep wound of the soul that becomes a stronghold if not healed. People bound by rejection struggle with identity, constantly feel unwanted, and are easily offended. Spirits of rejection, insecurity, and abandonment often cluster here.

5. Pride

Pride is perhaps the most dangerous bondage. It blinds people to their need for God, resists correction, and breeds rebellion. Demons of pride and self-exaltation attach to this stronghold and create walls that block the Spirit's work.

How to Identify Strongholds

As a minister, you must learn to discern when a person's issue is primarily a demon and when it is a stronghold of the flesh or soul. Often it is both. Here are some ways to identify strongholds:

Patterns of Behavior

If the same sin or struggle repeats over and over despite prayer and effort, it may be a stronghold. Addictions, cycles of anger, or recurring fear patterns point to entrenched bondage.

Emotional Triggers

If certain memories, words, or situations trigger strong emotional reactions, that can reveal a soul wound. For example, if someone explodes in anger whenever authority corrects them, rejection or pride may be the stronghold.

Lies and Beliefs

Strongholds are built on lies. If someone consistently believes, "I'm worthless," "No one loves me," or "I'll never change," you're dealing with a soul stronghold that needs truth to break it.

Demonic Manifestation

When strongholds are present, demons often manifest when you confront them. Fear, anger, or addiction may rise up as a spirit when exposed. This confirms that the bondage is both fleshly and spiritual.

Breaking Strongholds

Strongholds are not broken by willpower alone. They are broken by applying the truth of God's Word, repentance, renunciation, and deliverance.

Step 1: Repentance

Lead the person to repent for agreeing with the stronghold. Example:

"Lord, I repent for agreeing with anger and for letting bitterness control me. I turn from it now."

Step 2: Renunciation

Have them renounce the lie or agreement. Example:

"I renounce the lie that I will always be rejected. I declare the truth that I am accepted in Christ."

Step 3: Forgiveness

If the stronghold ties to wounds, lead them to forgive. Example:

"I forgive my father for rejecting me. I release him into Your hands."

Step 4: Breaking the Stronghold

Declare with authority:

"I break every stronghold of fear in this person's life in the name of Jesus."

"I tear down every lie of rejection and declare the truth of God's acceptance."

Step 5: Casting Out

Once the ground is removed, command the spirits to leave:

"Spirit of fear, your stronghold is broken. I command you and all your kingdom to go now in the name of Jesus."

Step 6: Filling With Truth

Finish by declaring Scripture:

"God has not given you a spirit of fear, but of power, love, and a sound mind."

"You are a new creation in Christ; old things have passed away."

Practical Ministry Examples

- Addiction — Lead the person to repent for seeking comfort in substances instead of God. Have them renounce the spirit of addiction. Break the stronghold of shame. Cast out spirits of addiction, bondage, and torment. Declare freedom and self-control.
- Fear — Lead them to repent for agreeing with fear. Break lies like, "I'm not safe." Lead them into forgiveness for those who caused trauma. Cast out spirits of fear, anxiety, and torment. Declare peace and boldness.
- Anger — Have them repent for agreeing with wrath. Lead them to forgive those who wronged them. Break inner vows like, "I'll never let anyone hurt me again." Cast out spirits of anger, violence, and rage. Declare gentleness and self-control.
- Rejection — Lead them to forgive those who abandoned them. Renounce lies of worthlessness. Break inner vows like, "I'll never belong." Cast out spirits of rejection and insecurity. Declare acceptance in Christ and belonging in God's family.
- Pride — Lead them to repent for self-exaltation. Break lies like, "I don't need anyone." Cast out spirits of pride and rebellion. Declare humility, dependence on God, and sonship.

A Word on Patience

Breaking strongholds is often a process, not a one-time moment. Some people are delivered quickly. Others must walk through discipleship, accountability, and renewing their mind. Don't get discouraged if it takes time. True freedom is worth the journey.

Bondages of the flesh and soul are some of the most common obstacles you will face in deliverance ministry. They may look different on the surface—addiction, fear, anger, rejection, pride—but at their core, they are strongholds built on lies and pain.

As a minister, your job is to expose those strongholds, lead people in repentance, break agreements, cast out the spirits attached, and then fill the person with the truth of God's Word. When you do, you will watch the most stubborn chains fall off.

Freedom is not just about casting out demons. It is about healing the soul, breaking strongholds, and restoring people into the fullness of Christ. And when that happens, deliverance becomes more than a moment—it becomes a lifestyle of victory.

Reflection Questions

1. This chapter teaches that many issues are not "just demons," but entrenched patterns of the flesh or wounds of the soul that demons attach themselves to. Why is it dangerous to treat every struggle as purely demonic—or purely psychological/fleshly? How does recognizing both dimensions lead to more complete and lasting freedom?

2. Strongholds are built on lies: "I'm worthless," "I'll always be this way," "No one wants me." Why do lies—especially identity lies—have so much power in shaping someone's behavior, emotions, and spiritual vulnerability? What Scriptures directly confront the most common lies people believe (fear, rejection, anger, addiction)?

3. This chapter emphasizes that breaking strongholds is often slow: repentance, renunciation, forgiveness, renewing the mind, and sometimes repeated deliverance. Why do you think God often chooses *process* instead of instant transformation? How does process produce deeper maturity, character, and long-term freedom?

15

OCCULT, WITCHCRAFT, AND GENERATIONAL CURSES

ONE OF THE MOST COMMON AND DANGEROUS OPEN DOORS TO demonic bondage comes through the occult, witchcraft, idolatry, and generational curses. These practices create covenants with darkness, often knowingly but sometimes unknowingly. They give demons legal ground not just in one person's life but in entire family lines.

If you want to minister deliverance effectively, you must be equipped to confront these strongholds. In this chapter, I'll show you how the occult and generational sin operate, how to identify them, and how to break them through the authority of Jesus Christ.

The Nature of Witchcraft and the Occult

The Bible is clear: witchcraft and occult practices are abominations to God. Deuteronomy 18:10–12 says, "There shall not be found among you anyone who practices witchcraft, or a soothsayer, or one who interprets omens, or a sorcerer, or one who conjures spells, or a medium, or a spiritist, or one who calls up the dead. For all who do these things are an abomination to the Lord."

The occult includes practices like:

- Witchcraft and sorcery
- Tarot cards, palm reading, astrology
- Ouija boards and channeling spirits
- Necromancy (attempting to contact the dead)
- New Age practices like crystals, energy healing, and spirit guides
- Yoga and meditation tied to false religions
- Idolatry and sacrifices to other gods

These things are not harmless games or cultural traditions. They are entry points for demonic spirits. People who dabble in them may not realize it, but they are making covenants with darkness that need to be broken.

The Spirit of Witchcraft

Witchcraft is not only about spells and rituals—it is a spirit. Galatians 5:20 lists witchcraft (sorcery) as a work of the flesh. But behind it is a demonic power that seeks to control, manipulate, and dominate.

The spirit of witchcraft works through:

- Control and manipulation. Trying to bend others' will.
- Domination. Using fear or pressure to subdue.
- Intimidation. Making people afraid to resist.

This is why Paul warned the Galatians, "Who has bewitched you?" (Galatians 3:1). Witchcraft clouds minds and leads people away from truth. In deliverance, you will often find witchcraft spirits connected to fear, control, rebellion, or the occult.

Idolatry and False Worship

Behind every idol is a demon. Paul wrote in 1 Corinthians 10:20, "The things which the Gentiles sacrifice they sacrifice to demons and not to God."

Idolatry is not limited to statues of wood or stone. Anything exalted above God becomes an idol: money, power, fame, even relationships. But in many cultures, idolatry also includes literal offerings to false gods. These acts form covenants with demonic spirits that must be renounced and broken.

Generational Curses and Patterns

Exodus 20:5 says that the sins of the fathers can affect the children to the third and fourth generation. This is not about God punishing children for their parents' sins—it is about the reality that sin patterns and curses travel down family lines until they are broken.

Common generational curses include:

- Cycles of divorce or broken marriages
- Patterns of addiction or alcoholism
- Mental illness and torment
- Premature death or chronic sickness
- Poverty and financial lack
- Occult involvement passed down

When you see the same pattern repeating across generations, you are often dealing with a generational curse. These curses are broken not by psychology but by the blood of Jesus.

How to Break Curses and Generational Patterns

Breaking curses requires intentional prayer and declaration. Here's the process I use:

1. Lead in Repentance

Repent not only for personal sins but also for generational sins. Example:

"Lord, I repent on behalf of my family line for every act of witchcraft, idolatry, and rebellion against You."

2. Lead in Renunciation

Have the person renounce every generational covenant. Example:

"I renounce every covenant made with darkness in my bloodline. I declare my only covenant is with Jesus Christ."

3. Apply the Blood

Declare that the blood of Jesus severs every generational chain. Example:

"By the blood of Jesus, I cut off every curse, every spirit, and every claim of the enemy over my family line."

4. Break the Curse

Speak with authority:

"I break every generational curse of addiction, poverty, and rejection. I declare these patterns end today in the name of Jesus."

5. Cast Out the Spirits

Command the spirits to leave. Example:

"Every spirit of witchcraft, every ancestral spirit, every generational demon—I command you to go to the pit now."

6. Declare Blessing

Replace the curse with blessing:

"I declare this family line is covered by the blood of Jesus. From this day forward, generational blessing flows in place of generational curses."

Practical Prayers to Break Inherited Spirits

Here are some sample prayers you can use with those receiving ministry. Lead them line by line so they can declare it themselves:

Prayer of Repentance and Renunciation

"Father, I repent for the sins of my ancestors and my own sins of witchcraft, idolatry, and rebellion. I renounce every covenant made with darkness in my family line. I declare my only covenant is with You, Jesus Christ."

Prayer of Breaking Curses

"In the name of Jesus, and by the power of His blood, I break every

generational curse over my life and my family. I cut off every spirit of addiction, poverty, rejection, infirmity, and death. These patterns end today."

Prayer of Deliverance

"I command every spirit that entered through generational sin to leave me now. Every ancestral spirit, every occult spirit, every demon of witchcraft—I bind you and cast you out in the name of Jesus."

Prayer of Blessing

"Father, I receive Your blessing in place of every curse. I declare freedom, health, joy, peace, and generational blessing over my life and my children. I belong to You, and my family belongs to You."

Ministering to Those Coming Out of the Occult

When ministering to people who have been deeply involved in witchcraft or the occult, patience and persistence are often required. These covenants can be deep, and spirits may resist.

Key things to remember:

- Be thorough. Walk them through every practice, every object, every ritual. Have them renounce each one.
- Destroy objects. Encourage them to burn or throw away occult items—tarot cards, crystals, idols, books, or jewelry. Acts 19:19 shows believers burning occult books publicly.
- Fill with truth. Teach them to replace lies and rituals with the Word and with worship.

- Stay in discipleship. People coming out of the occult often need ongoing mentoring and accountability.

Witchcraft, occult practices, idolatry, and generational curses are some of the most powerful open doors to the enemy. But they are no match for the cross, the blood, and the name of Jesus.

As a deliverance minister, you carry authority to break every curse, cancel every covenant, and set every captive free. Lead people in repentance, renunciation, and forgiveness. Apply the blood. Declare the curse broken. Cast out the spirits. And release them into generational blessing.

Remember: the power of Jesus is greater than every spirit of witchcraft. The cross has already triumphed. And through Him, you have the keys to enforce that victory in every life and every family line.

Reflection Questions

1. THIS CHAPTER MAKES IT CLEAR THAT OCCULT INVOLVEMENT— whether tarot, crystals, witchcraft, New Age, or contacting the dead—is not "harmless curiosity" but forms real covenants with darkness. Why do you think people are so easily drawn to these things today, even Christians? What spiritual hunger or wound are they trying to meet illegally—and how does the enemy capitalize on that desire?

2. JESUS BREAKS EVERY CURSE, BUT PEOPLE STILL EXPERIENCE generational patterns—divorce, addiction, mental torment, occult history, poverty. What patterns have you seen in families (yours or others) that clearly point to spiritual inheritance? How can someone discern whether a pattern is psychological, environmental, or genuinely spiritual in nature?

3. THIS CHAPTER EMPHASIZES THAT THE OCCULT, IDOLATRY, AND even inner vows create *legal rights* in the spirit realm. How does understanding the "legal" nature of the spiritual realm change the way you view repentance, renunciation, and breaking curses? Why is the language of covenant so important in deliverance?

16

RELIGIOUS, REGIONAL, AND TERRITORIAL SPIRITS

DELIVERANCE MINISTRY IS NOT ONLY ABOUT SETTING INDIVIDUALS free. The same spirits that torment people also work in systems, churches, cities, and regions. The Bible speaks of principalities, powers, rulers of darkness, and spiritual hosts of wickedness in the heavenly realms (Ephesians 6:12). These are territorial spirits—demonic powers that exert influence over groups of people, regions, and even nations.

In this chapter, I want to give you an understanding of three major categories you will face in broader deliverance ministry: religious spirits, regional spirits, and territorial principalities. Each requires discernment, intercession, and apostolic authority to confront.

Religious Spirits: Control and Counterfeit

One of the most destructive spirits you will encounter is the religious spirit. This spirit doesn't always make people look evil —it often makes them look spiritual. But it is a counterfeit spirit that produces control, legalism, pride, and counterfeit spirituality.

The Nature of the Religious Spirit

Religious spirits thrive where there is form without power. Paul warned in 2 Timothy 3:5 about people who have "a form of godliness but deny its power." Religious spirits promote:

- Legalism. Elevating rules and rituals above relationship with Jesus.
- Control. Using spiritual authority to dominate rather than serve.
- Pride. Trusting in knowledge, tradition, or appearance rather than grace.
- Counterfeit spirituality. Substituting religious activity for true intimacy with God.

This spirit opposed Jesus more than any other. The Pharisees, full of religious pride and control, resisted Him at every turn. Even today, religious spirits are some of the strongest enemies of revival and freedom.

Signs of a Religious Spirit at Work

- Resistance to the move of the Holy Spirit.
- Obsession with outward appearance, rules, or traditions.
- Harsh judgment toward others while excusing self.
- Pride in knowledge without true love.
- Fear of freedom, emotion, or supernatural power.

Breaking Religious Spirits

When ministering deliverance to individuals bound by religious spirits, repentance is key. Lead them to renounce pride, control, and legalism. Declare freedom into intimacy, grace, and the power of the Spirit.

On a corporate level, churches and ministries must be covered apostolically and guarded through prayer and teaching to resist religious spirits.

Regional Spirits: Influence Over Cities and Regions

The Bible gives clear examples of demonic influence over geographic areas. In Daniel 10, the angel spoke of the "prince of Persia" who resisted him, and the "prince of Greece" who would come. These were territorial spirits influencing entire empires.

Regional spirits are demonic powers assigned to cities, towns, or regions. They create atmospheres of bondage that affect the culture of a place.

Common Regional Strongholds

- Addiction. Cities where drug use or alcoholism dominates.
- Violence. Regions marked by gang activity, crime, or bloodshed.
- Sexual immorality. Areas where perversion and exploitation thrive.
- Poverty. Regions locked in cycles of lack and despair.
- Witchcraft. Towns or cities steeped in occult practices or false religion.

If you travel and minister in different regions, you will often sense these atmospheres. That is part of discerning of spirits on a territorial level.

Discerning Regional Spirits

When entering a new city to minister, pay attention to:

- Atmosphere. What do you feel when you step into the area? Fear? Darkness? Depression?
- Patterns. What sins or struggles dominate the community?
- History. What events shaped the spiritual foundation of the city? Wars, bloodshed, covenants, revivals, or occult roots?

Confronting Regional Spirits

Regional spirits are not cast out of individuals—they are confronted through intercession and apostolic authority. Prayer walks, fasting, worship gatherings, and corporate repentance are powerful tools. Churches must stand together in unity to confront regional bondage.

Territorial Principalities: Higher-Level Warfare

Above regional spirits are principalities—demonic rulers that operate over nations or territories. Paul described them in Ephesians 6:12 as "principalities and powers."

These spirits influence governments, economies, religions, and cultures. They are behind ideologies, false religions, and systemic oppression. For example:

- The principality behind idolatry in ancient Israel.

- The principality behind emperor worship in Rome.
- The principality behind Islam, Hinduism, or other world systems today.

These are not spirits you confront lightly or individually. They require corporate intercession, apostolic networks, and prophetic strategies.

The Role of Intercession

The most powerful weapon against religious, regional, and territorial spirits is intercession. Paul instructed Timothy in 1 Timothy 2:1–2 to make "supplications, prayers, intercessions, and giving of thanks... for kings and all who are in authority."

Intercession confronts spiritual atmospheres by appealing to the throne of God. When the church gathers to pray, principalities lose ground.

Strategies for Intercession

- Prayer Walks. Walk the streets of your city and declare freedom, binding the ruling spirits you discern.
- Corporate Fasting. Unite believers to fast for breakthrough over specific strongholds.
- Prophetic Declarations. Speak God's promises over your city or nation.
- Worship. Create altars of worship in regions dominated by darkness. Worship displaces the enemy's atmosphere.

The Role of Apostolic Covering

Territorial spirits are not confronted by lone rangers. They require covering and order. In Acts 19, the seven sons of Sceva tried to cast out demons without true authority, and they were overpowered. Authority flows through alignment with God and His order.

That is why apostolic covering is essential. Ministers who attempt to confront territorial spirits without proper alignment often find themselves under severe attack. But when you are submitted to godly leadership and rooted in the house of God, you carry covering that protects you and strengthens your authority.

In practical terms:

- Don't engage territorial warfare casually.
- Always operate in unity with your leaders and church family.
- Receive prayer covering when traveling to minister in new regions.
- Never let zeal outpace wisdom.

Practical Examples

- Religious Spirit. A church bound in tradition, resisting revival. Solution: teach grace, break control, and invite the Holy Spirit.
- Regional Spirit. A city marked by addiction and hopelessness. Solution: prayer walks, fasting, evangelism, and corporate repentance.
- Territorial Principality. A nation bound by false religion or corruption. Solution: apostolic and prophetic intercession, unity of churches, and long-term disciple-making.

Religious, regional, and territorial spirits are real, but they are not ultimate. Jesus is Lord over every principality and power. Colossians 2:15 declares, "Having disarmed principalities and powers, He made a public spectacle of them, triumphing over them in it."

As a deliverance minister, your first responsibility is to free individuals. But as you grow, God may entrust you with greater authority to influence atmospheres and regions. Approach this with humility, intercession, and apostolic covering.

Remember: the battle belongs to the Lord. Your role is to discern, pray, and obey. When the church rises in unity and authority, even territorial strongholds crumble. And when they do, entire regions experience the freedom and glory of God.

Reflection Questions

1. IN WHAT WAYS CAN A RELIGIOUS SPIRIT SUBTLY INFILTRATE A church or ministry—even one that believes in the Holy Spirit— and what signs would help you discern between genuine spiritual order and a counterfeit form of control, legalism, or pride?

2. THINK ABOUT YOUR OWN CITY OR REGION—WHAT SPIRITUAL atmosphere do you discern there, and what historical, cultural, or social factors might have opened the door to that regional spirit? How would a unified church practically confront that atmosphere using intercession, repentance, and evangelism?

3. WHY IS APOSTOLIC COVERING AND SPIRITUAL ALIGNMENT essential when confronting higher-level territorial principalities, and what dangers arise when individuals or ministries attempt to engage these realms outside of divine order and spiritual authority?

17

AFTERCARE AND DISCIPLESHIP

DELIVERANCE IS NOT THE FINISH LINE. IT IS THE STARTING POINT. Casting out demons is powerful, but if people are not rooted in discipleship and community afterward, they risk falling back into old patterns. Jesus Himself taught this in Matthew 12:43-45: when an unclean spirit leaves, it looks for rest, and if it finds none, it returns with seven others more wicked than itself. Deliverance without discipleship leaves people vulnerable.

That's why aftercare is one of the most critical parts of deliverance ministry. True freedom is not just about what leaves a person —it's about what fills them and who walks with them after.

Freedom Must Be Nurtured in Community

Freedom is not sustained in isolation. It is nurtured in community. God never designed us to walk alone. The early church understood this. Acts 2:42-47 describes believers devoting themselves to teaching, fellowship, breaking bread, and prayer. As a result, they grew strong and multiplied.

When someone experiences deliverance, they are often raw and tender. Their spirit is free, but their mind and emotions are still learning to adjust. They need a family around them who can encourage, support, and disciple them. Without that, the enemy will try to isolate and regain ground.

That's why I always emphasize: deliverance ministry must be connected to the house of God. Freedom is never meant to be disconnected from discipleship.

Spiritual Disciplines: Word, Prayer, Fellowship

One of the best ways to strengthen people after deliverance is to root them in spiritual disciplines.

- The Word. Teach them to read and declare Scripture daily. The Word renews the mind and replaces lies with truth.
- Prayer. Encourage them to develop a lifestyle of prayer, not just crisis prayer. Daily communion with God keeps the doors closed to the enemy.
- Fellowship. Plug them into regular gatherings with other believers. Fellowship provides encouragement, correction, and accountability.

Discipline may sound unglamorous compared to dramatic moments of deliverance, but it is the key to lasting freedom.

Accountability and Walking With Others

Deliverance is easier when someone has accountability. People relapse into bondage when they try to walk alone. That's why James 5:16 says, "Confess your trespasses to one another, and pray for one another, that you may be healed."

Encourage those who have been delivered to walk closely with mature believers who will check in, ask hard questions, and cover them in prayer. This isn't about legalism—it's about protection. Accountability is like guardrails on a road. It keeps people from veering back into the ditch.

If you are training ministers in deliverance, teach them to follow up. Don't just pray once and disappear. Call, text, and invite the person into deeper discipleship. Deliverance without follow-up is irresponsible.

The House Church Model

At SOZO Church, we've built aftercare into our house church model. Some people call them small groups, but for us, they are more than just a Bible study. Each house church is led by spiritually mature, submitted disciples of the house who are fully trained to minister all of Jesus' ministry—preaching, teaching, healing, deliverance, counseling, and discipleship.

When someone receives deliverance, I want them plugged into a house church quickly. Why? Because they will need more ministry, more prayer, and more discipleship. A Sunday service is powerful, but it doesn't provide the relational connection people need for ongoing freedom. House churches create a safe, consistent space for people to be nurtured.

Local Connection Matters

I often encourage people not to drive across town for discipleship when there's a house church nearby. If someone has to pass three house churches on the way to yours, that's not best for their long-term growth. They'll need ministry regularly, and they'll need a spiritual family close to them.

When someone gets free, plug them into the house church in their own community. That way they are rooted locally, surrounded by people who can walk with them daily, not just occasionally. Deliverance must be followed by discipleship, and discipleship works best when it is local and consistent.

Deliverance Is About Rooting People in the House of God

We must shift our thinking: deliverance is not just about casting demons out. It is about rooting people in the house of God. Freedom is sustained not only by what leaves but by where the person plants themselves afterward.

Psalm 92:13 says, *"Those who are planted in the house of the Lord shall flourish in the courts of our God."* Deliverance plants a seed of freedom. But flourishing requires being planted in God's house.

As ministers, our goal should never just be to empty someone of demons but to fill them with the Spirit and connect them to God's family. If we cast demons out but don't disciple, we've only done half the job.

Practical Aftercare Steps

Here are some practical steps you can take for effective aftercare:

1. Immediate Follow-Up. Within 24–48 hours, check in

with the person you ministered to. Encourage them, remind them of what Jesus did, and pray with them.

2. Scripture Assignments. Give them verses to meditate on daily, especially around identity, freedom, and victory.

3. Prayer Habits. Encourage them to pray daily, even short prayers of thanksgiving and declaration.

4. Community Connection. Plug them into a house church or discipleship group quickly.

5. Accountability Partner. Pair them with a mature believer who can check in regularly.

6. Encourage Testimony. Have them share what God did. Testimony seals faith and builds courage in others.

7. Ongoing Ministry. Remind them it's okay if they need more ministry. Freedom is often a process, not just one event.

Deliverance is powerful, but discipleship is what sustains it. Freedom must be nurtured in community, strengthened through spiritual disciplines, and protected by accountability. The house church model provides the best environment for this, because it roots people in local, relational discipleship.

Never forget: your role as a deliverance minister doesn't end when the demon leaves. It continues as you help people walk into maturity, identity, and calling. Deliverance is the doorway, but discipleship is the journey. And when people are planted in the house of God, their freedom will not only last—it will multiply into the lives of others.

Reflection Questions

1. How does the distinction between receiving deliverance and being discipled challenge the way many believers understand freedom, and in what ways might an absence of ongoing relational discipleship leave someone spiritually vulnerable even after a genuine encounter with God?

2. In what ways does being rooted in a local spiritual family—through teaching, fellowship, accountability, and shared life—shape a person's long-term transformation, and how might isolation or a lack of consistent community undermine the work God began in deliverance?

3. Considering the emphasis Jesus placed on what fills a person after deliverance, how should spiritual disciplines, accountability, and belonging to a house church reshape our understanding of "aftercare," and what does this reveal about the responsibility of both the minister and the one receiving ministry?

18

PROTECTING THE DELIVERANCE MINISTER

Deliverance ministry is powerful, but it is also demanding. When you step into the battlefield to confront the enemy, you must know how to protect yourself. I've seen too many ministers fall into burnout, deception, pride, or even open doors to the same spirits they were casting out.

The enemy would love to take out deliverance ministers. If he can't stop you from setting others free, he will try to intimidate, exhaust, distract, or corrupt you. That's why you must take your own protection seriously. Deliverance ministry isn't just about others getting free—it's about you living free yourself.

Spiritual Covering and Alignment

One of the greatest protections you have is spiritual covering. In Matthew 8, the centurion told Jesus, "I am a man under authority, having soldiers under me." Authority flows from alignment. If you're not under authority, you will not carry authority.

Why Covering Matters

- Protection. Covering keeps you from being an open target. Lone rangers are the easiest to pick off.
- Accountability. Covering keeps your character in check and ensures you don't drift into deception.
- Authority. True spiritual authority flows through submission. If you're under no one, your authority is compromised.

In my own house, I don't release people into deliverance ministry until they've gone through discipleship and shown they can live under authority. If you want to protect yourself, stay planted in the house of God, honor your leaders, and walk in alignment with the apostolic covering God has placed over you.=

Avoiding Burnout: Rhythms of Rest and Renewal

Deliverance ministry can be exhausting. Sessions can be long, draining, and emotionally intense. If you're not careful, you'll burn out. Jesus Himself often withdrew to lonely places to pray (Luke 5:16). If the Son of God needed rest and renewal, so do we.

Signs of Burnout

- Feeling numb or detached during ministry.
- Irritability or frustration toward people you're helping.
- Loss of joy or motivation.
- Physical exhaustion or illness.

Rhythms That Sustain You

- Rest. Take Sabbath seriously. Ministry without rest leads to collapse.
- Prayer. Stay filled daily. Don't just minister out of yesterday's oil.
- Community. Spend time with family and friends, not just in ministry.
- Boundaries. Learn to say no. You are not the Messiah—Jesus is.

Burnout is not a badge of honor. It's a sign you are out of rhythm with God's design. Protect yourself by staying refreshed.

Common Attacks on Ministers

The enemy knows if he can't stop you on the battlefield, he can try to undermine you off of it. Here are some of the most common attacks you'll face:

1. Fear and Intimidation

Demons often try to scare ministers, either by threatening, manifesting violently, or planting fear at night. Remember: fear is their weapon, not yours. Stand firm. Declare the Word. Remind yourself you are seated with Christ in heavenly places.

2. Pride

After a few powerful deliverance sessions, pride is a real danger. People will thank you, tell you how anointed you are, and demons themselves may say things like, "We hate you. Why are there so many angels with you?" Don't let it puff you up. Pride is the quickest way to lose protection. Stay humble.

Authority flows through brokenness and dependence on Christ.

3. Deception

Deliverance ministers who drift from the Word are vulnerable to deception. Some start chasing manifestations or listening to demons for revelation instead of staying anchored in Scripture. Don't build theology on what demons say. Test everything against the Word.

4. Lust and Moral Failure

Because deliverance ministry is so confrontational, the enemy often counterattacks in subtle areas. Lust, compromise, and moral failure are traps that destroy credibility and authority. Guard your purity. Walk in accountability.

5. Fatigue and Distraction

Sometimes the enemy doesn't hit with direct attack—he just keeps you busy, distracted, and drained. Protect your focus. Say yes to God and no to distractions.

Living Free Yourself

You cannot lead others into freedom if you are not walking in freedom yourself. Deliverance ministers must live in purity, humility, and authority.

Purity

Keep your heart and life clean. Confess sin quickly. Guard

your eyes, your thoughts, and your motives. Don't tolerate small compromises. Purity keeps your authority sharp.

Humility

Humility is not weakness. It is strength under submission. True humility says, "I carry authority because Christ lives in me, not because I am great." Stay low before God. Give Him glory for every victory.

Authority

Authority is not arrogance. It is confidence in Christ. You don't need to be timid or apologetic in deliverance. Speak with boldness because you know who you represent.

Renewal of the Mind

Keep renewing your mind with the Word. The enemy looks for cracks in your thinking. Replace lies with truth daily.

Practical Habits for Protection

- Daily Prayer and Word. Stay filled with the Spirit before you minister to others.
- Accountability Partners. Have trusted people who can ask hard questions.
- Debrief After Sessions. Pray with your team, release burdens to the Lord, and don't carry them home.
- Regular Rest. Take time off, enjoy family, laugh, and live life. Joy is one of your greatest protections.
- Worship Lifestyle. Worship shifts atmospheres and keeps your heart anchored.

- Covering. Stay aligned with your church, leaders, and apostolic covering.

Deliverance ministry is not just about casting demons out of others. It's about living free yourself. If you lose your purity, humility, or covering, you will eventually lose your authority.

Protect yourself by staying aligned, resting well, resisting pride, guarding purity, and living under authority. Remember: your greatest testimony is not just the demons you cast out but the freedom you live in.

Stay humble. Stay covered. Stay pure. And stay renewed. When you do, you'll not only last in deliverance ministry—you'll multiply freedom in others for decades to come.

Reflection Questions

1. IN WHAT WAYS DOES TRUE SPIRITUAL AUTHORITY FLOW FROM personal alignment, submission, and covering, and how might a minister's relationship to authority reveal unseen vulnerabilities that could later impact their purity, discernment, or effectiveness in deliverance ministry?

2. HOW DOES THE TENSION BETWEEN SPIRITUAL WARFARE AND personal well-being challenge deliverance ministers to cultivate rhythms of rest, humility, purity, and emotional health, and what does this reveal about the difference between carrying an anointing and carrying longevity?

3. CONSIDERING THE UNIQUE ATTACKS THAT TARGET DELIVERANCE ministers—fear, pride, deception, lust, distraction, burnout—what does it practically mean to "live free yourself," and how might the condition of a minister's inner life shape the spiritual atmosphere they carry into every session they lead?

CONCLUSION
SENT AS DELIVERERS

When God raised up Israel's judges, Scripture says, "Then the Lord raised up deliverers for them" (Judges 2:16). Those deliverers were not superheroes—they were ordinary men and women empowered by the Spirit of God to set His people free. In the same way, God is still raising up deliverers today.

You have walked through the foundations of deliverance ministry, the process of identifying open doors, the role of repentance, renunciation, and forgiveness, how to discern spirits, how to handle manifestations, how to bind, loose, and declare freedom, and how to protect yourself as a minister. All of this was written not so you would just have information, but so that you would step into the calling to set captives free.

Jesus said in Luke 4:18–19, "The Spirit of the Lord is upon Me, because He has anointed Me to preach the gospel to the poor; He has sent Me to heal the brokenhearted, to proclaim liberty to the captives and recovery of sight to the blind, to set at liberty those who are oppressed; to proclaim the acceptable year of the Lord." That anointing now rests on His body—the church. That means it rests on you.

Freedom Is the Children's Bread

When the Syrophoenician woman came to Jesus asking for her daughter's deliverance, He said, "It is not good to take the children's bread and throw it to the little dogs" (Matthew 15:26). Deliverance is the children's bread—it is the rightful inheritance of every believer. You have been called to bring that bread to hungry people.

But bread is not flashy. It is daily. It is consistent. It is basic sustenance. Deliverance ministry is not about building your name—it's about feeding God's people with the freedom that belongs to them.

The Balance of Humility and Authority

As you minister, never forget the balance: you are called to walk in bold authority and deep humility at the same time.

- Bold authority means you don't back down from demons, strongholds, or intimidation. You know who you are in Christ, and you speak with confidence.
- Deep humility means you never let deliverance become about you. You don't boast in manifestations or in your power. You boast in Christ alone.

Authority without humility leads to pride and a fall. Humility without authority leads to timidity and ineffectiveness. But together, humility and authority make you a true vessel of the Deliverer.

Deliverance Is Part of the Great Commission

In Mark 16:17–18, Jesus said, *"These signs will follow those who believe: In My name they will cast out demons; they will speak with new tongues; they will take up serpents; and if they drink anything deadly, it will by no means hurt them; they will lay hands on the sick, and they will recover."*

Casting out demons is not optional—it is part of the Great Commission. Too often the church has treated deliverance as rare, extreme, or unnecessary. But Jesus put it at the very front of the list. If you believe, you are called to this.

The Great Commission is not just about preaching and baptizing. It is about discipling nations, which includes freeing people from the bondage of the enemy. You cannot disciple someone while leaving them in chains.

Rooting People in the House of God

You've heard me say it throughout this book: deliverance is not just about eviction—it is about discipleship. Freedom must be rooted in community, in the Word, in prayer, and in the house of God.

If you cast out demons but do not connect people to the family of God, their freedom will be short-lived. But if you cast out demons and then disciple them into Christ's body, their freedom will last and multiply.

Remember, your role is not just to empty people of darkness but to fill them with Christ and plant them in His church. That's how deliverance turns into transformation.

Living as a Deliverer

Finally, this ministry is not just about what you do for others—it's about how you live yourself. You cannot lead people where you have not gone. If you want to minister freedom, you must live free.

Stay submitted. Stay pure. Stay humble. Stay in the Word. Stay in prayer. Stay covered. Keep your joy. Protect your family. Walk in rest. Refuse pride.

Demons will try to lie, intimidate, and accuse. They will try to pull you into fear or arrogance. But when you walk daily in intimacy with Christ, their words carry no weight. Remember: you are seated with Him in heavenly places (Ephesians 2:6). That throne is higher than any demonic throne.

A Final Charge

I want to leave you with this charge: Go and set captives free. Don't overcomplicate it. Don't make it about you. Don't chase manifestations. Simply walk in the authority of Christ, apply the blood, lead people into repentance, renunciation, and forgiveness, and declare freedom.

Preach the gospel. Heal the sick. Cast out demons. Make disciples. Build the house of God. Do it all with love, humility, and boldness.

And when you see freedom come—when the addict is sober, when the tormented mind is at peace, when the broken family is restored, when the oppressed are filled with joy—give Jesus all the glory. He is the Deliverer. You are His vessel.

Closing Prayer

"Lord Jesus, thank You for calling us to be Your hands and feet. Thank You for entrusting us with the ministry of deliverance. I pray for every reader—that they would walk in purity, humility, and authority. That they would be protected under covering. That they would feed Your sheep with the bread of freedom. And that through them, many captives would be set free.

Holy Spirit, fill them now with fresh boldness and wisdom. Guard them from pride, deception, and burnout. Surround them with angels of protection. Root them in Your house. And send them out to proclaim liberty to the captives and the opening of the prison to those who are bound.

In Jesus' name, Amen."

RESOURCES & APPENDICES

This section is designed to give you practical tools that you can use immediately in ministry. While the earlier chapters built your foundation and equipped you with understanding, these resources are here to provide language, structure, and quick reference so you can minister with clarity and confidence.

Prayers and Declarations

These are sample prayers you can lead people through during sessions. Use them as a guide, but don't become mechanical. Always listen to the Holy Spirit.

Prayer of Repentance

"Lord Jesus, I repent for agreeing with [name the sin: fear, lust, anger, addiction]. I turn away from it, and I choose Your ways. Wash me in Your blood and cleanse me from every sin. I receive Your forgiveness and declare that I am free."

Prayer of Renunciation

"I renounce every lie, vow, and covenant I made with [name the spirit or practice: witchcraft, rejection, lust, fear]. I break agreement with it in Jesus' name. My only covenant is with Jesus Christ, my Lord and Savior."

Prayer of Forgiveness

"Lord, I choose to forgive [name the person]. I release them from my judgment. I let go of the bitterness, anger, and pain I've carried. I give them to You, and I bless them. As I forgive, I receive Your healing and peace."

Prayer to Break Generational Curses

"Father, I repent for the sins of my ancestors and my own sins that opened the door to curses. In the name of Jesus, and by the power of His blood, I break every generational curse over my life and my family. I cut off every inherited spirit and declare freedom for me and my descendants."

Deliverance Command

"I command the spirit of [name] and all its kingdom to leave now and go to the pit, in the name of Jesus Christ."

"I bind you, spirit of [name]. Repeat after me: 'I, [spirit's name], bind myself to all my kingdom, and me and all my kingdom go to the pit now.'"

Declaration of Freedom

"Whom the Son sets free is free indeed. I am free by the blood of Jesus."
"No weapon formed against me shall prosper."
"I am a child of God, filled with the Spirit, and covered by the blood."

Ministry Protocols and Checklists

Deliverance should be powerful, but also safe, accountable, and Spirit-led. These protocols will help you structure sessions with wisdom.

Before a Session

- Pray and prepare yourself (Word, prayer, worship).
- Ensure at least two ministers are present (lead and helper/witness).
- Create a safe, private space without distractions.
- Review intake or history if available.
- Ask the Holy Spirit for discernment.

During a Session

- Begin with prayer and set the atmosphere.
- Have the person confess Christ as Lord.
- Lead them through repentance, renunciation, and forgiveness.
- Address legal rights as they come up.
- Use short, sharp commands when casting out demons.
- Keep the focus on Jesus, not the manifestations.
- Check if more spirits remain ("I command the next highest-ranking spirit to come forward").

- Release healing, peace, and the infilling of the Holy
  Spirit.

After a Session

- Pray blessing and protection over the person.
- Encourage them to rest in God's presence.
- Give Scripture assignments and prayer declarations.
- Connect them to a house church or discipleship
  group.
- Debrief with your team in private.

Forms and Tools

Having practical tools helps bring order and accountability
to ministry. Here are examples you can adapt for your context.

Intake Form (Sample)

- Name: _____
- Age: _____
- Contact Info: _____
- Church Affiliation: _____
- Brief history of struggles (check all that apply):

- ☐ Addiction
  - ☐ Anxiety/Depression
  - ☐ Anger/Violence
  - ☐ Occult involvement
  - ☐ Abuse/Trauma
  - ☐ Nightmares/Torment
  - ☐ Sickness/Chronic Pain

- Have you received ministry before? □ Yes □ No
- Do you want to follow Jesus wholeheartedly?　□ Yes □ No

Consent Form (Sample)

"I understand that this ministry session is offered as a prayer-based service for spiritual freedom. I consent to receive ministry in Jesus' name, and I release the ministers from any liability. I understand that ultimate freedom comes through Christ and walking in His Word."

Signature: _____ Date: _____

Notes Template

- Date: _____
- Ministers present: _____
- Main issues addressed: _____
- Key repentance/renunciations: _____
- Spirits cast out: _____
- Scriptures given: _____
- Next steps/aftercare: _____

Scriptures for Freedom

Here's a quick-reference list of passages you'll use often in deliverance.

Authority in Christ

- Luke 10:19
- Mark 16:17–18
- Ephesians 2:6

Victory of the Cross

- Colossians 2:14–15
- 1 John 3:8
- Revelation 12:11

Freedom in Christ

- John 8:36
- Galatians 5:1
- Isaiah 61:1–3

Weapons of Warfare

- 2 Corinthians 10:4–5
- Ephesians 6:10–18
- Hebrews 4:12

Identity in Christ

- Romans 8:37
- 2 Corinthians 5:17
- 1 Peter 2:9

Keep these Scriptures close—you'll use them in prayer, in ministry, and in teaching those who've just been set free.

Closing Word on Resources

These tools are here to serve you. Use them as guides, but don't let them replace dependence on the Holy Spirit. No checklist, prayer script, or form can substitute for His leading. But when paired with His presence, these resources can keep your ministry safe, accountable, and fruitful.

Remember: order protects freedom. Structure strengthens power. And the Word of God ensures victory every time.

ABOUT THE AUTHOR

Tom Cornell is the Senior Leader of SOZO Church in Washington state, founder of Walk in the Light International and SOZO Network. Tom is married to his beautiful wife Katy and lives in the Puget Sound area with her and their three kids. He has been in ministry pastoring and teaching the body of Christ since 2008.

He has a passion to see the body of Christ moving from people with an orphan mindset to that of sonship; equipping the body to do the work of Jesus resulting in seeing the Kingdom of God manifested here on earth.

www.ingramcontent.com/pod-product-compliance
Lightning Source LLC
LaVergne TN
LVHW052027080426
835513LV00018B/2197